MINDFULNESS MEDITATIONS *for* ADHD

MINDFULNESS MEDITATIONS for ADHD

*Improve Focus,
Strengthen Self-Awareness,
and Live More Fully*

MERRIAM SARCIA SAUNDERS, LMFT

ROCKRIDGE
PRESS

For general information on our other products and services or to obtain technical support, please contact our Customer Care Department within the United States at (866) 744-2665, or outside the United States at (510) 253-0500.

Rockridge Press publishes its books in a variety of electronic and print formats. Some content that appears in print may not be available in electronic books, and vice versa.

Interior and Cover Designer: Monica Cheng
Art Producer: Janice Ackerman
Editor: Andrea Leptinsky
Production Editor: Ruth Sakata Corley
Production Manager: Riley Hoffman

Illustration: © Basia Stryjecka/Creative Market

Paperback ISBN: 978-1-63878-086-1
eBook ISBN: 978-1-68539-697-8

R0

For my brother, James J. Sarcia,
and our father, James F.
You are my sunshine.

Contents

Introduction

If you had told me years ago that someday I would write a book on meditation, I might have laughed at you. Not that I didn't value meditation—in fact, quite the opposite. Since discovering in my youth that a beloved teacher was a practicing Buddhist, I'd been fascinated by the concept. Over and over, I tried to develop a meditation practice, searching like Goldilocks for just the right fit.

During college, I joined my teacher's Buddhist sect and practiced. I lived in Japan, where I visited the great Shinto temples. I went on yoga retreats, women's retreats, and shamanic retreats with sweat lodges. I tried tai chi and chi gong. In true attention deficit hyperactivity disorder (ADHD) form, I moved from one shiny new meditative object to the next and discovered the same problem each time: it was just so gosh darn difficult, impossible even, to sit still and focus on . . . nothing.

Just miles from my house in Northern California is a serene meditation center called Spirit Rock. It's nestled in golden grassy hills away from the hustle and bustle—the perfect place to gather and ground oneself. Spirit Rock has welcomed many renowned mindfulness experts, and I've had the fortune of hearing wise words in many dharma talks. After listening to these talks, when it was time to meditate, I'd try for a few minutes. Unsuccessful, I'd invariably slip outside and spend the remaining meditation time walking quietly around the grounds. I thought I was cheating. Failing. Meditation was not for me.

Then in 2007, my father developed lung cancer. It was inoperable, stage 4, and he was told that, at best, chemotherapy could reduce the tumor size, but he should have no expectation of remission. Undeterred, my father found an old book, published in 1920 by French psychologist Émile Coué. Dr. Coué believed the mind could heal the body, and he instructed his patients to meditate earnestly on

the mantra, "Every day, in every way, I'm getting better and better."
With nothing to lose, my father began a devoted practice of this
mantra meditation. After months of chemotherapy and relentless
positivity that his mind would cure him, my father's final scan showed
that his tumor had, in fact, completely disappeared. Of course, we'll
never know what part the mantra actually played, but he believed it,
and that was enough for me.

This was my first true understanding not only of the gift of
meditation but also of the fact that it had many faces besides sitting
and thinking of nothing. Faces, in fact, that often target the very
symptoms consuming my life as a psychotherapist who treats, lives
with, parents children with, and writes about ADHD.

Meditation for those with ADHD is not a painful impossibility. It
can be done successfully and with great impact. This book will give
you examples of the different faces of meditation—short and long,
sitting and walking, writing and imagining—all aimed at helping you
concentrate, regulate your emotions, calm your body, and increase
self-compassion so that every day, in every way, you can get better
and better.

CHAPTER ONE

MINDFULNESS, MEDITATION, and ADHD

You may be reading this filled with excitement to try something new. Or perhaps you're skeptical and worry that with your squirmy body and wandering mind, meditating is out of reach. Meditation doesn't have to be quiet and serious, and it's not done only by people who do yoga and have a rich, spiritual understanding of the word *dharma*. (If that's you, then welcome.) Although it's true there can be a mastery to meditation, that's not the goal of this book. I hope you'll find these exercises helpful, accessible, and, dare I say, fun. Meditation *can* be for you, too.

What Is Mindfulness?

Today, the buzzword *mindfulness* is everywhere, casually tossed about as something everyone should understand and embody. But phrases like, "Mindful eating is good for you," or "Bring a mindfulness to your breath" may leave you scratching your head as to exactly what mindfulness is and why it's so important.

If you look up mindfulness online, you'll likely find the definition coined by professor Jon Kabat-Zinn, who studied under Buddhist teachers and then integrated their concept of mindfulness into the Western scientific world via his Mindfulness-Based Stress Reduction program at the UMass Medical School clinic. He states, "Mindfulness is awareness that arises through paying attention, on purpose, in the present moment, nonjudgmentally."

In other words, being mindful means noticing what's happening at this very moment—how this book feels in your hand, how the aroma in the air around you smells, whether your neck is tense, or if you're already bored—without scrutiny, negative self-talk, or judgment.

We all have a jumble of thoughts pinging around our brains. Many of those thoughts are judgments, cravings, and a sense that life is less than it should be—not exactly rewarding thoughts. The Buddhists call this chatter our "monkey mind," as if our thoughts were mischievous monkeys swinging from tree to tree. We also have a tendency to go through our day on autopilot, unaware of how our bodies feel or how our minds are wandering or whispering to us their fears and concerns.

In Buddhism, mindfulness meditation, or Vipassana, aims to quiet the monkey chatter in our brains with a judgment-free, bare awareness of present-moment thoughts, feelings, and sensations. Despite its early connection to Buddhism, mindfulness is far from a religious practice. It is, however, a practice—one of reminding yourself to stop and notice what's going on inside and around you without judgment, like a stockroom clerk who inventories a store's products without evaluating them. In the next sections, we'll learn why practicing mindfulness can make a difference with your ADHD and your life as a whole.

Why Mindfulness Works

If you've picked up this book, perhaps you have some issues with executive functioning (EF), such as impulsivity or difficulty focusing or planning. Maybe you feel three steps behind everyone, always forgetting something and feeling anxious, like you just don't get the rules of life. You may be considering alternative strategies to cope, but fear that there's no way you could meditate. The good news is, mindfulness can help, because even the small act of noticing your moments and re-centering your thoughts and feelings on a daily basis can physically shift your brain's circuitry. Restless, inattentive patterns may be replaced by more effective ones, allowing you to focus, find calm, get mentally organized, and enjoy a new sense of well-being.

What Is Meditation?

When people think of mindful meditation, many envision sitting cross-legged with palms up and eyes closed while chanting *ommmmmm* for hours. They wouldn't necessarily be wrong. But that's not all meditation is. In a nutshell, if mindfulness is a state of being where the mind's monkey chatter is noted with a gentle curiosity and politely dismissed, then meditation is a means to get there.

The paths to this place of gentle awareness are many, and none of them involves desperately trying to keep the mind clear at all times. For a restless mind like mine—and perhaps yours, too—this is good news. Some meditations are long and require sitting; others are quick and can be done anywhere. Clear-mind meditations aim to improve attention and bring clarity by emptying the mind. Other meditations focus on increasing compassion and loving-kindness—these are called open-heart meditations. Movement meditations use the body to increase awareness, but mantra or sound meditations use chanting, phrases, and tones to induce a sense of well-being. Mindfulness meditations train us to invite curiosity to our inner and outer worlds with that same ultimate destination of calm.

Why Meditation Works

The saying "You can't teach an old dog new tricks" does not apply to the human brain. Neuroscience has shown that the brain has a plasticity to it, which means that with concerted thought, it can stop using long-entrenched neural pathways that aren't beneficial and adopt new, healthier patterns. These new patterns can improve how we think about ourselves and others, but there's more—they can even shift our cardiovascular, immune, and central nervous systems for the better.

It isn't a question of simply wishing your brain to change. Change requires work. After years of brain imaging and clinical trials, the results are pretty irrefutable: working at meditation changes your brain in some key areas. But it doesn't take long. In just eight weeks of practicing mindfulness, study after study has shown that meditation can improve working memory, protect the brain and heart as it ages, make it easier to fall asleep, help regulate emotions, and improve mental clarity, generosity, and the ability to focus on the task at hand. Phew! That is a long list of benefits, many of which greatly impact executive functioning and ADHD.

How to Meditate

Whether you meditate for 30 seconds or 30 minutes, your mind *will* wander. That's perfectly fine. The objectives are to focus on an anchor—usually your breath but sometimes a visual, mantra, or body part—and to notice when your mind has left the building. When this happens, gently bring your awareness back to your anchor and restart, without chiding yourself for having let it drift.

Meditation doesn't have to be done with closed eyes while seated in the lotus position in a quiet location. Some of the meditations in this book will call for that, but most can be done almost anywhere— seated at your desk or while standing in line at the grocery store. In fact, the more you practice meditating, the more you'll find that mindfulness permeates all areas of your life and then simply becomes part of who you are.

CHAPTER TWO

ADHD *and the* BRAIN

People living with attention deficit hyperactivity disorder often share common challenges. Some people with ADHD struggle to pay attention to things that are boring and bring too much attention to things they adore. Others struggle with physical and mental restlessness and an inability to pause before acting. Many struggle with a little of all of the above.

Brain Deep Dive

ADHD is characterized by three main issues: inattention, hyperactivity, and impulsiveness. To be diagnosed as an adult, five out of nine symptoms must have been present before age 12, occur in at least two settings, and interfere with life.

We know from brain imaging, such as fMRI and PET scans, that the area of the brain called the prefrontal cortex works a bit differently in people with ADHD. The prefrontal cortex is where our higher-level thinking, or executive functioning, happens. It's where we organize and plan, and where we regulate our impulses, emotions, and attention. It's what gives us a sense of space and time and where we remember things we've just heard. In a person with ADHD, the prefrontal cortex doesn't light up as brightly when performing certain executive functions, and, until adulthood, it is often a few years behind in size and development. It's thought this is due to a lack of neurotransmitters, namely dopamine and norepinephrine, whose job is to stimulate the brain into action. When the prefrontal cortex doesn't receive these neurotransmitters, it's as if we're asking it to drive cross-country on one tank of gas. It just can't go the distance. This is why many with ADHD opt for stimulant medication to help produce neurotransmitters.

Research shows that in addition to medication, there are other means to help the prefrontal cortex. These include regular exercise, yoga, martial arts, cognitive behavioral therapy, and, you guessed it, meditation.

Although these meditations may prove helpful in your quest to overcome executive functioning challenges, they should by no means be thought of as a substitute for treatment. Seek the advice of a medical professional about a well-rounded treatment plan that may or may not include medication and psychotherapy.

Mindfulness for ADHD

The first time I was invited to Spirit Rock, it was for a dharma talk by renowned mindfulness expert Jack Kornfield. I nearly bolted when I was told it would be followed by a long meditation. The thought of sitting still and focusing only on my breath sounded boring and painful. People with ADHD have notoriously wandering minds, so how could I be expected to sit still with a blank one—and why should I? At the time, I thought all I needed was therapy and medication, not meditation!

The go-to treatment for ADHD is a combination of medication and cognitive behavioral therapy (CBT). CBT strives to reorient the ADHD brain's endless and distorted monkey chatter. By cultivating an awareness of rigid, negative thoughts, such as *I never do anything right* or *Don't bother unless it's perfect*, we can reframe those thoughts as more positive, realistic ones, like *Sometimes I do things right* and *Maybe less than perfect is okay*. These reframes help shift our sense of self so we can see the possibilities of trying new, more productive strategies for executive functioning struggles.

An increasing number of studies show the efficacy of meditation as a treatment supplement for ADHD. But getting there can feel like a challenge. For people with ADHD, the notion of "paying attention on purpose" may seem futile, as it did to me years ago when I began this journey. If the "cure" is the very thing we struggle with, how are we supposed to change anything, right? But imagine this: You're planning to sit at your desk to write. You go to get your coffee and notice you're running low on milk, so you add it to the grocery list on your phone. While you're on your phone, you see an email notification, so you check your emails and answer a few. An online ad reminds you that you need a new mattress, so you slip down that rabbit hole for a while. When you finally sit at your computer to write, your neck aches from reading on your phone, making it harder to focus. You get up frequently to stretch and each time you do, you're irritated by your inability to get the work done.

You don't have time to meditate, and how is it supposed to help with all that anyway?

Amazingly enough, it can—and not by preventing you from getting your coffee, checking emails, or buying a new mattress, or by forcing you to strap yourself to your chair to work. In that scenario, you'd set the stage by picking a short morning meditation from this book and breathing into it before that cup of coffee. While enjoying your coffee, you might find yourself noticing its nutty aroma and warmth in your hands, more than you would on other days. Your commitment to acting mindfully means that adding milk to your grocery list is done with intent, rather than on autopilot, allowing you to choose to check emails later. When you sit at your desk, you pick from one of the meditations that centers you, before starting a task, and spend a few moments breathing and visualizing. While writing, when you lose focus, you notice the necessity for a break and allow it, without judging yourself for needing to do so. You may or may not get more work done. But at the end of the day, your choices were intentional, and you feel calmer and have more self-compassion.

Just as ADHD treatments look different for each individual, so will mindfulness practices. For some, it may be a mindful walk in nature. For others, a long meditation after a dharma talk by Jack Kornfield could be just the thing.

Meditation and ADHD

Every day, in every way, I'm getting better and better.

It's fascinating that intentional words, repeated to the self over and over, can change one's physical makeup. Here's why it works: we know with scientific certainty that experiences taken in by the senses and processed in the brain affect us physically. This is largely to keep us alive. If the brain senses a threat, it immediately drops control from the critical-thinking prefrontal cortex and diverts it to the limbic system. The limbic system's job is to pump cortisol and adrenaline into the body to increase the heart rate and get the large muscle group ready for fight or flight; this is very helpful if you're about to be attacked by a lion.

But what if all you're facing is a verbal attack by your boss? Or your own inner critic? The modern-day problem with our brains is that they haven't evolved to completely discern the difference between an impending lion attack, our inner critic, and the wrath of our boss because we missed a deadline. This is where positive mantras and meditation come in handy. As psychology professor Kristin Neff explains, self-criticism triggers the body's threat defense system in the same way an impending lion attack does. So when the attacker is our own monkey chatter—say, shame over forgetting an appointment or frustration over losing our keys—our brains and bodies respond with a similar cortisol and adrenaline rush. This may give our sluggish ADHD brains a good jolt and thrust us into action, but it has unhealthy long-term consequences for our bodies. Relying on this jolt can create too much chronic cortisol, which, in turn, can cause inflammatory disease, dampen the immune system, and damage the thyroid.

People with ADHD specialize in self-criticism. In an article in *Clinical Psychiatry News*, Dr. Michael Jellinek estimates that by the time a child with ADHD reaches the age of 12, they've heard upward of 20,000 more criticisms than their neurotypical peers. The monkey chatter has been implanted in your head by the world around you, and the uphill battle against it is an understandable one.

It isn't surprising, therefore, that ADHD rarely walks alone. According to the organization Children and Adults with ADD (CHADD), an estimated 47.1 percent of people with ADHD are also diagnosed with an anxiety disorder. Anxiety is characterized by excessive worrying, and excessive worrying triggers a similar cortisol release response in the brain.

Additionally, many people with ADHD report a co-occurrence of rejection sensitive dysphoria (RSD). RSD is the extreme perception of being rejected or criticized. It can feel very real and cause tremendous emotional pain. People with ADHD have a sharp radar for criticism but often misunderstand others' intentions and assume they are being rejected, even if they aren't.

The good news is, according to neuroscientist Richard Davidson, overall well-being is a learnable skill, rooted in our flexible brain circuitry. It can be improved with practice, much like how you get better at playing a musical instrument the more you practice. The more we engage those brain circuits with mindfulness-based activities, such as positive mantras, the more we disrupt the brain's critical narrative and the greater our overall sense of well-being becomes. Another good reason to consider meditation!

Now let's talk about how it works: When you breathe slowly and deeply, you send a signal to your brain that it's not necessary to create lots of oxygen and pump lots of blood to the large muscle groups to prepare for fight or flight. When you slow down and notice your distractions, sensations, and emotions with acceptance and compassion, you send a similar signal to the brain that all is well—otherwise, you'd be on high alert, looking outward for danger, or scrutinizing inward for something physically wrong. Negative self-talk can trigger the threat defense system, but self-acceptance and compassion cause almost the opposite in the brain—the limbic system releases oxytocin, which creates calm, reduces cravings, and promotes sleep. This area of the brain is also responsible for understanding social cues and forming attachments, which helps in combatting rejection sensitivity. Win, win!

When will I start to feel better?

"Feeling better" is a relative term that means something different for everyone. For you, it may mean an increased sense of calm or a greater ability to sustain attention. Perhaps you hope to be less forgetful or manage big emotions without exploding. Chances are, even in a small way, you'll feel better with your first deep breath as it sends calming signals to your brain. But realistically, the more you practice, the sooner you may begin to experience an overall change in how you feel.

How do I know when I'm meditating and not just sitting there?

If you're just sitting there, congratulations! At least you're there, attempting the exercise. As with most new ventures, we almost always fumble and feel inept until we've practiced. Follow the steps in the exercises, change things up however you need, and above all notice, notice, notice—without judging whether you're "doing it right." There is no right or wrong way to meditate.

Am I supposed to think?

You will think. And that's absolutely fine. Mindfulness isn't about staying with your anchor—it's about returning to your anchor. When your thinking drifts drastically from the meditation at hand, gently return your attention to your breath, sound, or visual, and continue.

What if I always fall asleep?

Falling asleep happens sometimes, typically due to the body reaching a relaxed state, coupled with the mind wandering away from its meditation anchor. But if you're falling asleep every time, you might not be getting enough sleep at night. Or you might be meditating at a very relaxing time of day. Double-check your sleep hygiene (see page 129), and experiment with meditations at different times of day. If all else fails, you could set an alarm.

What is the best meditation position?

Sitting still for 20 minutes might not be possible right away, and that's okay. Although sitting with a straight spine is best for keeping your brain activated, the best meditation position, at first, may be the one you're most comfortable with.

What if my mind wanders?

If your mind wanders, and it almost certainly will, practice noticing that it wandered and gently return it to your meditation. You may need to do this over and over. That's okay. In fact, it's great. This practice of returning to your focus may eventually generalize to your life outside the meditation and help you develop a habit of pausing before acting.

When is the best time of day to practice?

Ideally, mindfulness will become second nature and won't be limited to certain times of day. In the beginning, though, choose whatever time of day works for you—you're more likely to practice if it fits your schedule. You may want to try different times before settling into one routine.

How much time is needed?

There is no magic number of minutes that classify you as legitimately meditating. Due to the nature of ADHD, it may make sense to start with a short amount of time and work your way up. Even people who don't have ADHD find it helpful to start small.

Can I meditate while walking or running?

Absolutely! Some of the meditations in this book will specifically call for that; others you can adapt to do while moving.

Do I have to meditate every day?

Hopefully you'll see the benefits of even the simplest meditations, and it won't seem like a chore you *have* to do. As with any new skill, practicing daily will make it easier and more enjoyable and effective in the long run.

Am I focusing too much on not focusing?

If you're asking this question, then possibly, yes. With most of the meditations in this book, you will be asked to focus on or visualize *something*—not nothing. If you drift away for a moment, gently return. If you're doing a clear-mind meditation, let your mind do what it will without constantly trying to keep it clear. Again, the idea is to notice your mind has wandered and just bring it back. Don't be too hard on yourself.

Is five minutes a day worth it?

Even 30 seconds a day is worth it! If this book is in your hands, then you're probably willing to give it a try. Take the leap and see. You can even practice mindfulness while brushing your teeth and washing your face at night if you're not ready for a more committed practice.

CHAPTER THREE

PREPARE *for* MEDITATION

The old adage "Practice makes perfect" does not serve those of us with ADHD very well. We often get so caught up in the notion of perfection that it stops us from ever starting the task. Author Malcolm Gladwell hypothesizes that it takes 10,000 hours of repetition to master a task. But luckily, mastery isn't necessary to begin seeing the benefits of a regular mindfulness practice.

Best Habits and Practices

The true definition of *practice* is to do something habitually. With my clients who have ADHD, I often discuss the benefits of setting up routines. Routines make it easier to remember important tasks and events, transition from one activity to the next, and plan for the future—all things ADHD likes to mess with. If you're not already doing so, implementing a routine may help with overall ADHD management. Then add at least a few minutes of a meditative practice into that routine so you have a shot at remembering it. If transitions are difficult, employing a transitional object—like using the same sitting pillow or nodding to a treasured collectible—can signal to your brain that it's time to settle into meditation. If you stray from your routine, don't give up. Just like re-anchoring your wandering mind in a meditation, you can re-anchor your routine. Tomorrow is another day!

If you exercise regularly, you've felt the benefits. You feel the positive rush as endorphins flood your system. You may feel lighter on your feet and more clearheaded. Perhaps you sleep better at night. But you might also remember a time when exercise wasn't a part of your daily routine and how getting into it was difficult, even painful. If you play a musical instrument, you might remember how hard it was when you first started—how difficult it was to connect the notes to the fingering, how slowly it came, how awful it sounded! Now, though, perhaps playing music lulls you into a meditative state that is as second nature to you as breathing.

A meditation practice is like that. It won't necessarily be easy at first. But the more you stick to it, the easier and more beneficial it will become.

How to Use This Book

Here are a few helpful tips to get you started.

Do what works for you. There's no one right way to meditate. Every meditation, unless it specifies otherwise, will tell you to get into a comfortable position and ask you to breathe. Your comfortable position is up to you—eyes open or closed. For lengthier meditations, it's a good idea to minimize distractions. You may want to use earplugs or, conversely, try soothing music, since many people with ADHD focus better with a secondary sensation in the background. If music is too distracting, try meditating using a fidget spinner or something relaxing to touch. In other words, use whatever helps facilitate your experience. Remember, there's no right or wrong way to meditate.

Use this book however you like. This book is divided into sections that focus on different goals. You may choose to begin with your greatest need. Or you may choose to move through the meditations in order, so that after 100 days of committed daily practice, you've tried every single meditation. Earmark your favorites to return to as part of your ongoing mindfulness practice. You can even make a game of it by randomly selecting a different page each day. If you're new to meditation, I recommend starting with Breathing 101 (page 22) and Mindfulness 101 (page 24). Then you may want to move on to Calm the Body meditations (chapter 5), as they focus more on the basics.

Start with an intention. Since you're working on mindfulness, when you sit down to each meditation, set your intention by stating it aloud, something like, *Now I am going to work on calming my mind.*

Enlist your phone to help. It might seem counterintuitive for people with working memory issues to have to read and remember multiple steps of a brand-new meditation, when simply remembering to meditate in the first place is a challenge. In this case, your phone is your friend. Set a calendar appointment with an alarm as a reminder to meditate. Then, read the steps aloud while recording them into your phone. Play it back when you're ready. (Record the title of the meditation and its page number for easier reference, and make each meditation its own recording file.) This way, you'll be able to access your meditations not only during your scheduled time but also when you're in line at the DMV, or when you need a quick break at work. Some people dislike the sound of their recorded voice, but chances are, the more you listen to it, the more you'll get over that.

Above all, don't give up. With enough trial and error, you'll find the right meditation fit for your beautiful monkey mind.

CHAPTER FOUR

CALM *the* MIND

Distraction—it happens to everyone. But if you have ADHD, it happens to a potentially impairing degree. You're going to get distracted. It's inevitable. But what you do afterward is key. Will you attack yourself, quit, get frustrated, or just notice it? The best thing is to simply notice it. Gently bring yourself back and start over. The meditations in this section are geared toward calming your scattered monkey mind and strengthening its ability to focus, remember, plan, and accomplish—without beating yourself up along the way. The exercises are ordered in such a way as to prepare you for tasks, so you may want to practice these in order.

Breathing 101

I'm going to teach you to breathe. That may seem silly because you do it automatically and without thinking all day long, but that's the point. Breath is the anchor for every meditation in this book. When your mind wanders, your breath will bring it back. When you are stressed, your breath will calm you down. If mindful meditation is a treasure chest, your breath is the gold inside.

STEPS:

1. Find a comfortable position. Sitting is ideal, but you may lie down or stand on your head if that's how you feel most relaxed.

2. Close your eyes, or if you want to keep them open, keep them soft, rested on a single spot just in front of you. Relax your face.

3. Set your intention for the next few minutes by repeating, *I am going to learn to breathe.*

4. Inhale through your nostrils until you can no longer fill your lungs. Hold for two counts, then exhale through your nostrils. That is one breath cycle.

5. Repeat step 4 again, this time paying close attention to how the air feels as it fills your nose. Is it warm or cold? Does it tickle? Are your nasal passages clear or a bit stuffed? If you have narrow airways, feel free to breathe through your mouth.

6. Now count as you breathe, maintaining an awareness of the air entering and leaving your lungs: *In, two, three, four. Hold, two, three, four. Out, two, three, four.*

7. Complete three breath cycles while counting.

8. Then complete three more breath cycles while counting, inhaling through your nose and exhaling through your mouth.

9. If you like, try making an audible breath sound as you exhale.

10. Next, move your awareness to your chest as you inhale. Feel it rise and then fall. Notice the sensation at the bottom of your lungs as you fill them to the brink. How do your ribs feel? Your back?

11. After several cycles, move your awareness to your belly. When people are stressed, they tend to breathe only into their chest. Imagine a balloon in your belly that fills as you inhale. Place a hand over your belly button and push against it as you inhale. Notice if it's easier to breathe into your belly or chest. Which feels better?

12. Notice if you placed any judgment on yourself during this breathing exercise. Did the fact that you read that people who are stressed tend to breathe into their chest create a narrative? Were you able to do this for 10 minutes? If not, did you get frustrated? Bored? If so, that's all okay. Let it go, take another breath, and try again tomorrow.

When you do this exercise again in the future, you may breathe through your nose or mouth into your chest or belly—whichever suits you comfortably. Try to stay rhythmic, paced, and aware.

Congratulations! You now know how to breathe.

Mindfulness 101

🌿 *Mindfulness Exercise*　　　　　　　　🕐 *5 to 10 minutes*

You learned to breathe in the last exercise. Now I will teach you how to stay present. Our minds typically wander to the past or the future more often than they remain in this exact, fleeting moment, as we're often trying to remember something or decide what to do next. This exercise will ask you to let go of the past and future—for just a moment. After all, this is the moment at hand, and it is a gift.

STEPS:

1. Assume a comfortable position.

2. Set your intention: *I am going to practice being mindful for the next few minutes.*

3. Bring your attention to any sensations you feel in your body. Adjust any uncomfortable feelings as necessary.

4. Begin breathing deeply, but don't count—just breathe. Be aware of your breath; follow it in and out.

5. Where is the focal point of your breath—nose, chest, or belly? Bring your attention to this place.

6. Notice the top of the inhalation, just as it becomes an exhale at a place of your choice.

7. Let the breath be as long or as short as feels natural. Feel it, follow it.

8. At some point, your mind will wander away from your breath. Gently escort it back.

9. Continue escorting your mind back to your breath as necessary for as long as you can.

10. When you're ready, open your eyes or lift your gaze. Note any sensations in your body and any sounds around you. Notice any judgments, thoughts, or emotions you feel. Take one more breath and let them go.

No matter how long you practiced, from 30 seconds to 30 minutes, you were present, living in the moment.

I Am Here

⚘ *Mindfulness Exercise*   ⏱ *Less than 5 minutes*

One of the biggest struggles for people with attentional issues is distraction, especially when faced with an unexciting task. It can be easy to procrastinate by checking social media or following a shiny new object that pops up in an online ad. This mindfulness exercise will help center your mind, body, and intentions as you endeavor to complete the task at hand.

STEPS:

1. Settle yourself wherever you're meant to begin this task. Get into a comfortable position.

2. Once settled, physically tap the hard surface nearest you: your desktop, the kitchen sink, a book cover. As you tap, say out loud, "I am here."

3. Set your intention: *I am going to do X for Y amount of time.*

4. Complete 3 deep breath cycles, focusing on your intended task.

5. Now, begin your task.

6. If you find yourself wandering off task, go back to step 2 and start again.

Pomodoro Meditation

You may already be familiar with the Pomodoro Technique, a standard strategy for managing ADHD symptoms. The idea is to set a timer for a short amount of time and commit to focusing only on a specific task. If a distracting thought arises during this work time, you quickly write it down to deal with later. When the timer buzzes, take a quick break. Then, repeat the process. Here we will practice a mindful Pomodoro meditation. Start with a short amount of time, with the goal of increasing it as you strengthen your mindfulness muscles.

STEPS:

1. From a comfortable position, set your intention.

2. Set your timer for 5 minutes.

3. Do either the Mindfulness 101 (page 24) or Breathing 101 (page 22) meditation for the set amount of time.

4. When you notice a distracting thought, imagine it being written down in a nearby notebook, and refocus on your meditation.

5. When the timer buzzes, reset it for half the time you meditated. Stand, stretch, look out the window. Do whatever you like—including writing down any distractions if need be.

6. Set your timer again for the same amount of time as in step 2, then repeat steps 3 through 5. Continue this pattern for as long as you like.

7. Each day, try to add time to your meditation segment and take a break for half the amount of time you meditated. As you strengthen your mindfulness muscles, you can begin to decrease the length of your breaks.

The Three-Legged Stool

⚘ *Mindfulness Exercise* ⏲ *10 to 20 minutes*

If you think of mindfulness as a stool, imagine the three legs that stabilize it are the breath, the body, and sound. If you feel wobbly at any point in the day, this exercise will help you stabilize your focus and emotions.

STEPS:

1. In a comfortable position with your eyes closed or open, complete 1 mindful breath cycle and set your intention.

2. For 5 cycles of deep breathing, listen to the sounds around you. Are they far away? In the room with you? Notice the type of sound and describe it without judgment.

3. Continue for another 5 breath cycles, this time paying attention to your breath. Notice if you're breathing rapidly or slowly, deeply or shallowly. Is the air warm or cold as it enters? Feel it in your nose or mouth, filling your chest, raising your navel.

4. Next, move your attention to your body for another 5 breath cycles. Notice if you feel energized or tired, warm or cold. With an exhale, let go of any tension. If you ache somewhere, notice it and move on.

5. If your mind strays from your body, your breath, or sound, gently return it and refocus on that leg of the stool.

6. Try cycling through the 3 legs over and over for 5 breath cycles at a time, working your way up until you eventually reach 20 minutes.

The Finish Line

Sometimes starting a project feels impossible, often because the finish line seems too far away. Consequently, the bill pile remains untouched, the closet unorganized, and the email unsent. This meditation will help you visualize your desired outcome, whether it's checking off your to-do list or planning the family vacation, so taking the first step will not feel so daunting.

STEPS:

1. Find a comfortable position. You may want to close your eyes.

2. Notice any tension in your body and release it with 5 deep, mindful breaths.

3. Visualize the task you've been avoiding.

4. Notice if your body tenses. Relax that area.

5. Now visualize completing the task. Notice the sounds, smells, and colors around you. Who is with you? What are you touching as you finish this task? Picture yourself smiling with the task complete.

6. Notice the positive emotions you feel. Let them cover you like a blanket.

7. As your body relaxes, covered in positivity, slowly bring yourself back to now.

8. When you're ready, take another deep breath, then open your eyes.

9. Now take the first step to complete the task.

Mindful Reading

Many people with attention issues find reading difficult. With the meditations in this book, you may be impatient to start and frustrated that you have to read through the steps before beginning. You just want to get to it. For this exercise, you'll read the steps slowly and mindfully so that reading this book becomes part of your journey, instead of a hurdle to getting to your destination.

STEPS:

1. Get into a comfortable position with this book in your lap.

2. Take 3 mindful breaths with your eyes open or closed, and set your intention.

3. Read the rest of this meditation aloud and very slowly. Savor the words, as if you can taste them.

4. Say the word *e-nun-ci-ate*. Feel how the N vibrates in your nose. Feel the tickle of the C and the crunch of the final T.

5. Say the word again, take in a breath, then say it again.

6. Read this next line quickly, like you might normally: *May I give myself patience in this new journey.*

7. Now read the sentence as if each word were its own sentence.

    May
    I
    Give
    Myself
    Patience
    In
    This
    New
    Journey

8. Read the sentence again, emphasizing the *I* and *myself*: *May I give myself patience in this new journey.*

9. Now read it again, this time emphasizing the word *patience*.

10. Play with the sentence, reading it slowly and differently each time. Which way of reading gives the sentence more power?

11. Finish with a few minutes of mindful breathing.

Generalizing tip: *As you read during your day, challenge yourself to do so mindfully and slowly, taking in the words and their meanings, like you do when you inhale a mindful breath.*

Embrace Your Executive Function Constellation

✵ Self-Compassion Exercise   ⏱ *15 minutes*

This meditation is a visualization that may be helpful when you're feeling particularly down on yourself. Review the following short list of executive functioning issues:

- Difficulty sustaining attention
- Difficulty completing tasks
- Difficulty starting tasks
- Frequent forgetfulness
- Frequent instances of losing things
- Messiness
- Disorganization
- Sensitivity
- Moodiness/irritability/volatility
- Restlessness
- Poor sense of time
- Talkativeness/frequent interrupting
- Impulsivity/riskiness
- Money mismanagement

STEPS:

1. Check or circle the issues on the list that you identify with. This is your EF constellation.

2. Now get into a comfortable position, close your eyes, and set your intention: *I will spend the next 15 minutes on self-compassion.*

3. Take 3 deep, mindful breaths, keeping your awareness on your breath.

4. When you're ready, shift your focus. Imagine a starry night sky.

5. Imagine your EF list as a cluster of stars. Now see yourself casting your EF constellation into the night sky with the other stars.

6. All the stars above make up who you are. This EF constellation is just a few among them. You didn't ask for this constellation. It's part of your biological makeup, like the constellation of your hair, eye, and skin color.

7. Imagine your constellation twinkling back at you. It doesn't shine any more or less than the rest; it just is.

8. Notice what comes up for you emotionally.

9. Imagine yourself breathing in the light from the stars. As you breathe out, let go of any judgments you may notice about this constellation.

10. When you're ready, open your eyes and carry on.

Touch a Bubble with a Feather

✿ Compassion Exercise   *① 10 minutes*

Mindfulness master Pema Chödrön suggests that during a meditation, "When things come up, touch them very lightly, like a feather touching a bubble." This meditation will help you bring a mindfulness to your distractions without being harsh on yourself and strengthen your brain's ability to avoid distractions throughout your day.

STEPS:

1. From a comfortable position with your eyes closed, begin mindful deep breathing cycles.

2. Stay connected to your breath, its sound and sensations.

3. When a distraction joins you, name it with one word. *Kids. Work. Friend. Travel.*

4. While thinking of the word, envision lightly touching a feather to a bubble, without intending to pop it.

5. Go back to your breath.

6. Each time a distraction comes, name it, and touch the bubble in your mind. Continue with this visualization for the duration of your practice.

Generalizing tip: During the day, be as gentle with yourself for getting distracted as you would be touching the bubble. Label the distraction, and envision touching the bubble. Then let it go.

Be Alarmed

Sometimes at the end of the day, I realize I've spent hours in my chair writing without moving. My new smartwatch has two terrific features that help me combat this. The first is a "Time to Stand" reminder, which pings me if it senses I haven't moved in a while. The second is a breathing app that I adore. It pulses my wrists rhythmically, coaching me to breathe as I watch an abstract blue flower open and close. If you have access to this technology, I recommend it. If not, you can make your own by setting "stand up" and "breathe" alarms.

STEPS:

1. When your alarm goes off, physically change whatever position you were in. If you were sitting, stand. If you were standing or moving, sit.

2. With your eyes opened or closed, practice mindful breathing for up to 5 minutes.

3. When you finish your breath cycles, before returning to your task, do a self-check: was the task you were just on an intentional one, or did you get distracted and go down a rabbit hole?

4. If you got distracted, make a mindful choice to complete the rabbit-hole task or circle back to your original intention.

5. You may wish to set an alarm for your rabbit-hole task to ensure you return to the original intention.

6. When the alarm goes off, say goodbye to the rabbit-hole task, breathe, and start anew.

Say It, Don't Stray It

✻ Mindfulness Exercise   ⏲ *20 minutes*

This is a focused breath meditation that helps train you to notice and let go of your distractions. This meditation can be as short or long as you like; however, the lengthier it becomes, the more effective it will be in helping you manage distractions.

STEPS:

1. Grab a writing utensil or phone to record the meditation.

2. In a comfortable position with your eyes open or closed, begin your focused breath meditation.

3. When your mind wanders, say the thought out loud: *I'm thinking of* _____. (If you're using pen and paper, quickly write it down.)

4. Bring your mind back to your breath and continue.

5. Each time a thought pops up, say it out loud or write it down, then return to your meditation. Try this for as long as you can, up to 10 minutes.

6. When you've finished, go back through the meditation and count the number of distractions you felt. How important were your thoughts? Was there something pressing, or were the monkeys simply at play?

7. After listening to or reading your distractions, do a final focused breath meditation for 2 minutes. With each exhale, let go of the distractions you spoke aloud or wrote down.

8. Each time you try this meditation, count the number of times you speak or write down a distraction in the same amount of meditation time. Over time, you may see this number decrease.

What's Your Problem?

⚐ Cognitive Exercise   *⏱ 20 minutes*

When you're faced with a problem, a technique called "green lighting" can be helpful. Green lighting is a way of collecting all solutions, making space for out-of-the-box ideas in an ADHD mind where sometimes only perfection is welcome. For this exercise, you'll need pen and paper or a computer (with the internet turned off).

STEPS:

1. At your computer or with pen and paper, focus on the problem at hand. Write it down in detail.

2. With your eyes open or closed, get into a comfortable position.

3. Begin a mindful meditation, focusing on your breath. When your mind wanders, invite it to move away from the thought and gently bring it back to your breath.

4. Meditate for 15 minutes.

5. When you've finished your meditation, go back to your computer or pen and paper.

6. Start writing down all the possible solutions to your problem, even the most ridiculous, impossible ones—anything. Keep writing until you're completely out of ideas.

7. Once you've finished, review your list and circle the top five best possible solutions.

Generalizing tip: If you thought of multiple solutions, use that as your intention for your next meditation. Meditate on one solution and write down what appeared for you. You may be surprised at how your mind tackled the problem.

The Scenic Route

⚹ Concentration Exercise　　　　　　⏱ *15 minutes*

According to Stanford neuroscientist Andrew Huberman, there are two types of vision—focal and panoramic—and the type we use controls how alert we are and how stressed or calm we feel. When we use focal vision, we send signals to the autonomic nervous system that there's a reason to stare, and we may be in danger. Conversely, panoramic vision sends the opposite message to the body, allowing for calm. If we hyper-focus, we may be using focal vision, keeping our bodies stressed, making it difficult to transition out of the task. The next time you find yourself hyper-focusing, try this meditation. For best results, find a place with an expanded view of your surroundings.

STEPS:

1. Find a comfortable position with an expanded view, preferably of the horizon. A park or beach is ideal, but looking out your window will work, too.

2. Keep your eyes open and your gaze soft.

3. Look at a point on the horizon but try not to fix your gaze on it. Take a few mindful breaths.

4. Dilate your stare so you take in not only that point but also all that's around it.

5. With your head perfectly still, extend your gaze to include the far reaches of your peripheral vision. This may bring your vision inside the room or to the person sitting next to you on the park bench.

6. Make a mental note of the things in this scene and any movements as you continue with your mindful breath cycles.

7. Note whether it's easy or difficult to rest your gaze this way, letting go of any judgment.

8. When you're ready to finish, close your eyes and complete 3 mindful breath cycles.

Generalizing tip: This exercise can also work in reverse. If you're struggling to focus, a few minutes of focal vision can help jolt you out of that fuzzy brain feeling. Try staring at a single point on the wall while completing several mindful breath cycles, then attempt your task.

A Mindful Habit

For this exercise, choose something you do repeatedly that's a struggle. Maybe you constantly lose your keys or overschedule yourself. Maybe you get impatient with your children or check your phone at the dinner table. This meditation will help you move through this habit more mindfully, giving you an opportunity to make a different choice.

STEPS:

1. Get into a comfortable position and close your eyes.

2. Begin breathing mindfully.

3. When you're ready, imagine the issue that challenges you. Picture yourself doing that habit. Note what emotions come up. Are you tense anywhere in your body?

4. With your next exhale, let the tension and emotion connected to that habit float out on your breath.

5. Now imagine yourself again, this time as you slowly and mindfully move through the visualization. What are you touching? Who is with you? Where are you?

6. In this moment, can you make a more deliberate choice? Can you proceed differently than usual?

7. Breathe into this new and more mindful way of action.

8. Continue with your mindful breath cycles until you are ready to open your eyes.

Staring Meditation

Charles Darwin could apparently spend hours on end staring at nature. Some say that was the secret to his incredible mind. He had a relentless curiosity, always peeling back the layers of things he noticed by examining their details and asking himself questions about them. This meditation aims to improve concentration and mindfulness by practicing examination the way Charles Darwin did.

STEPS:

1. From a comfortable sitting or standing position no more than five feet from a wall, try to find a small mark on the wall.

2. Affix your gaze steadfastly to the mark.

3. As you stare, begin breathing mindfully, keeping your eyes locked on the mark on the wall.

4. Soon, your vision may begin to blur, or your eyes may involuntarily begin to focus elsewhere.

5. As this happens, start to ask yourself questions about the mark.

6. How big is it? What color is it? Is it high or low on the wall? Does it have smooth or rough edges? What shape is it? Does it resemble anything?

7. Practice coming back to these questions every time your mind strays, and continue breathing mindfully until you're ready to end the meditation.

Generalizing tip: If you're having trouble focusing, take a moment to breathe and ask yourself a few questions about what you notice about the thing you're supposed to be focusing on. This may help you better attend to it.

CHAPTER FIVE

CALM *the* BODY

In the book *The Body Keeps the Score*, trauma psychologist Bessel van der Kolk states, "We have the ability to regulate our own physiology, including some of the so-called involuntary functions of the body and brain, through such basic activities as breathing, moving and touching." Simply put, calming your mind calms your body, and the opposite holds true, too. The meditations in this section will help you understand the connection between mindfulness, breath, and body.

Body Scan 101

⚜ *Mindfulness Exercise*　　　　　⏱ *20 minutes*

Our bodies often provide our first clue that something is upsetting us. We tend to carry our stress in the same place—head, neck, shoulders, or abdomen—and feeling tension there can be an important signal. Some of us ignore these physical sensations, but others become overly focused on the discomfort. Body scanning is a progressive physical check-in that promotes relaxation and awareness. Learning to become aware of your body as it relates to your stress is a step toward managing that stress, as you either choose to breathe into and relax the tension or notice and simply sit with the discomfort.

STEPS:

1. This meditation is ideally done lying down, as gravity helps anchor your body awareness. If think you might fall asleep, you can choose another position or lie on a hard surface. I like to keep my hands palms down on my abdomen, as it helps connect me to my breath, but you may place them at your sides, too.

2. Starting with your toes and feet, notice how they feel. If you feel nothing, does bringing awareness to them cause an urge to wiggle your toes or arch your feet? Inhale all the way down to your toes.

3. Moving up your body, feel the weight of your legs against the ground. Are they restless? Cramping? Relax and breathe into your legs.

4. Next, check in with your pelvic area and up to your abdomen. With your hands on your abdomen, notice how they rock like a small boat on the wave of your breath. Relax any tension in your belly.

5. Move up to your chest. Sense your heart beating steadfastly inside. Can you feel it? Feel the area expand as you inhale and relax as you exhale.

6. Let your shoulders drop and feel the weight of your arms. Notice any sensations. Are you warm or cold? Do you itch anywhere? Notice and resist the urge to move. Breathe into your arms.

7. Gently rotate your neck and release any tension or aching.

8. Feel the back of your head on the ground. Tighten your face, pucker your lips, squeeze your eyes shut, then relax.

9. Finish by doing several breath cycles, noting, without judgment, any sensations or residual tension that remain in your body.

Generalizing tip: This is a great practice when you're having trouble falling asleep. In addition to bringing awareness to your body, try actively tensing each area and then relaxing it.

Sitting 101

You can be mindful in any physical position—sitting, standing, lying down, walking. Purists, however, say that meditation is most effective when done seated. Sitting with your spine straight, your shoulders back, and your head balanced above your neck provides the optimal balance between relaxation and focus. According to a study by San Francisco State University's Erik Peper, sitting up straight also increases one's ability to elicit positive memories. The following exercise will explore four different seated positions. Try them all now, even if you think you already know your preference, as going through these motions will help anchor your body.

CHAIR

1. Sit in a chair and place your feet flat on the floor with your hands in your lap. Scoot forward in the chair, keeping your knees directly over your ankles.

2. Let your shoulders drop down and away from your ears. Pull them back comfortably. Relax your middle.

3. Your spine should be tall and not hunched. Imagine a string that comes out of the top of your head and runs down your spine; as it's gently tugged, your head and spine line up.

4. Begin 5 minutes of mindful breathing.

CROSS-LEGGED

1. If you can, move to the floor and sit in a cross-legged position. You may wish to sit on a cushion. Place your hands, palms up

or down, on your knees. If it's difficult to keep straight posture here, simply notice it.

2. Begin 5 minutes of mindful breathing.

BACK TO THE WALL

1. While sitting cross-legged on the floor if you can, scoot to a wall to support your back. Keep your shoulders touching the wall.

2. Place your hands, palms up or down, on your knees, noting how it feels to support your back with the wall.

3. Begin 5 minutes of mindful breathing.

KNEES

1. If you can, kneel and then sit back on your feet. This may be the most or least uncomfortable position. Take care if there is undue stress on your knees. Try placing a cushion under your buttocks.

2. Begin 5 minutes of mindful breathing.

In all four positions, note how your body feels. Are your ankles or knees stressed? Do your shoulders curl forward? If you have the urge to reposition, note it and resist the urge. Is there one position that makes it easier to focus on your breath?

Generalizing tip: If you're seated for a good part of the day, shifting your body in your chair regularly and standing to take a few steps can reset your spine to a healthy posture, which translates to better concentration and overall well-being.

Misogi

Misogi is a Japanese word to describe the Shinto practice of purifying the mind, heart, and soul of negativity. This is done by cleansing the body with icy cold water. Don't worry—for this exercise, using your imagination works just as well! This can help you become more alert and reduce stress.

STEPS:

1. This exercise is best done barefoot. Stand or sit. Feel the ground beneath your feet. Be sure to have enough room around you to raise your arms.

2. With your arms at your sides and your eyes open but soft, start a mindful breath cycle.

3. On your next inhale, raise your arms with your palms up and cup your hands together over your head.

4. With your hands cupped, keeping in pace with your exhale, lower your hands in front of your face, chest, and belly, and then let them rest at your sides. This is the cleansing movement.

5. Repeat step 3, but when you inhale and raise your arms this time, imagine you are gathering positive, cleansing water.

6. As you exhale and lower your arms, imagine that water pouring over you, pushing out the stress caused by your problem and filling you with clarity and calm.

7. Inhale, imagining again that you're gathering pure, calming water, then cleanse yourself of the negative stress with your exhale.

8. Repeat this movement for the suggested 10 minutes, or for as long as it is helpful.

Goldilocks and the Four Positions

✲ *Movement Exercise* ⏲ *15 minutes*

Your ability to be mindful and calm may differ depending on where you are and how you're positioned. For this exercise, you will shift positions, giving you an opportunity to notice differences within the same meditation.

STEPS:

1. Start in any seated position. Do 3 minutes of mindful meditation. Spend the first minute noticing your breath, the second minute scanning your body, and the third minute scanning your mind.

2. Now stand. Place your feet hip-width apart and plant your feet firmly; let your hands drop to your sides. If you feel compromised standing, lean against a wall. Do 3 minutes of mindful meditation, like in step 1.

3. Do a 3-minute walking meditation (page 156). Ideally, this is done outside. You can do it inside your home if you can do so without being disturbed.

4. Next, lie down for 3 minutes and repeat the meditation from step 1. If you're worried about falling asleep, set an alarm.

In which position did you feel the most relaxed physically, the most calm emotionally, and the most alert cognitively? Keep this in mind next time you have a specific aim with meditation, and perhaps choose that position for your day's practice.

My, What Lovely Fingers You Have

⚬ Concentration Exercise　　　　　　*🕐 5 to 10 minutes*

Our minds will often find ways to distract us when we're in pain. Distraction makes the pain easier to tolerate, especially if it's a chronic emotional or physical one. This exercise looks at how your mind is aware of and perceives discomfort.

STEPS:

1. Sit in a chair with your shoulders back and your spine straight, then with your fingers pointing left, raise your left arm until it's level with your shoulder.

2. Slowly turn your head to the left and look at the back of your hand. Inhale.

3. As you breathe in and out, try to keep your arm steady and your gaze fixed.

4. Notice if and when this feels difficult. Do your muscles feel heavy? Does your arm shake? Can you breathe through the discomfort?

5. Look at the back of your hand. Notice the skin, the knuckles on your fingers. Can you see the tips of any fingers? Are your nails long or short? Continue examining your hand while you breathe, noticing if your gaze wanders.

6. Remember, you are simply noticing what your hand looks likes and how your arm feels.

7. When you're ready, lower your arm.

8. Complete several breath cycles, and reflect on whether it was easier to keep your arm up while you were examining your hand.

Make a Fist

⚶ *Compassion Exercise*   ⏱ *10 minutes*

What happens when we stop resisting our experiences and emotions and accept them for what they are? It isn't easy! We fill ourselves with "shoulds," and when things go differently, we can be very critical of ourselves. This meditation is the physical embodiment of that inner experience. Its aim is to bring mindfulness to your inner critic.

STEPS:

1. While seated or standing, tuck your fists into your chest.

2. Form tight fists and squeeze as hard as you can, holding the squeeze for 3 breath cycles.

3. Notice what comes up. Does your face tighten? Does your breathing pace increase? Do you feel tense inside as well as in your fists? This represents the tension in your body when your inner critic has words with you.

4. Now let your arms drop and shake them out. Relax your shoulders. Raise your arms lightly in front of you, keeping your palms up in a receiving position.

5. How does this position feel?

6. Place one hand over the other palm and bring your hands to your heart, imagining you are pulling light and love toward you.

7. Take a moment to feel the gentle pressure of your warm hands on your heart.

8. This position represents self-acceptance and compassion for who you are. Carry this throughout your day, and if your inner critic pipes up, place your hands on your heart and breathe to remind you of how you want to feel.

Flatten a Gold Coin

Sometimes it feels like our desires and our brains are diametrically opposed. We want to finish something, stay on task, listen closely, remember instructions—but our brains have other plans. This meditation makes those opposing forces physical, but also helps you calm down any agitation that might have resulted from things going differently than you desired.

STEPS:

1. Standing with your feet shoulder-width apart, complete 3 mindful breath cycles.

2. Cup your hands together, imagining that in them you carry a gold sphere the size of a tennis ball, and raise them to your chest.

3. After another breath, press your palms together as if you're trying to flatten the gold sphere into a large coin. Press tightly! Make sure you don't lurch your shoulders or head forward.

4. Continue pressing, imagining the large coin breaking into smaller ones, as you cycle through 3 breaths.

5. On the final exhale, push the breath out hard as you release your hands and throw the gold coins onto the floor.

6. Roll your neck and shoulders to release any tension, and take one more breath.

You Deserve a Hug

⁂ *Stress Management Exercise*   ⏲ *5 minutes*

Our bodies respond to touch by releasing oxytocin, which makes us feel loved, and by reducing cortisol, thus decreasing stress and calming the cardiovascular system. The next time you feel high-intensity emotions, try giving yourself a soothing hug. Your mind might know it's your own arms around you, but your body won't know the difference.

STEPS:

1. When you're upset, stressed, or down on yourself, close your eyes and wrap your arms around your chest.

2. Inhale into the embrace and imagine you're inhaling loving, caring tenderness.

3. Acknowledge the uncomfortable feelings you're having in this moment. Tell yourself it's okay.

4. You may wish to rub your arms as you hug yourself or gently rock back and forth.

5. Breathe into the squeeze. As you exhale, notice how your body feels. If there's physical tension, squeeze your arms tighter as you inhale and release the tension on the exhale.

6. Check in with your previously big emotions. Do they feel different after this hug? Don't judge the feelings—just notice that they exist and that you may be struggling in this moment.

7. Remind yourself that struggling is a part of life and offer yourself another gentle arm rub.

8. Take several more mindful breaths, and when you're ready, release your hug.

Sensory Overload

☆ Mindfulness Exercise ⏲ *10 minutes*

Some people with ADHD have heightened sensitivity to things like light, sounds, and touch. Recognizing which sense may be heightened can help you understand why you sometimes have more intense emotions in certain circumstances. This mindfulness, in turn, can bring you self-compassion when that happens.

STEPS:

1. Try to find a bustling spot outside—the mall, a restaurant, the park, a busy street.

2. Complete several mindful breath cycles.

3. With your eyes open, run through your five senses, spending a minute or two on each. What do you see, hear, and smell? Does your skin tickle? Is your mouth dry? Does it have a particular taste?

4. As you focus on each sense, note what comes up physically and emotionally. Do you tense up anywhere? Do you feel agitated, sad, or angry, or do you feel light, calm, and content?

5. If you felt anything negative with one of the senses, recognize that this sense might be heightened. A sensory trigger may be why you feel inexplicably avoidant or irritated in some situations.

6. You can try this exercise with other potential triggers: food, clothing, or bright lighting, for example.

Generalizing tip: The next time you face a situation where your sensory trigger might get tripped, take a few mindful breaths and set your intention to note the discomfort and allow it to pass without judgment.

Water You Looking At?

✼ Concentration Exercise   ⏱ *5 minutes*

"The rays of the sun, when focused upon an object by means of a sun glass, produce a heat many times greater than the scattered rays of the same source of light and heat. This is true of attention." This quote and the following adapted meditation are from a 1918 book by Theron Dumont called *The Power of Concentration*. This meditation aims to improve not just mental concentration but also muscular concentration. I find that it makes a great mindfulness meditation (and it strengthens my arms!).

STEPS:

1. Fill a glass half full with water. While seated or standing, hold the glass and extend the hand that holds it in front of you. Raise your arm, keeping it straight, until it reaches shoulder height.

2. Fix your gaze on the water and keep your arm steady so the water line moves as little as possible.

3. Begin your mindful breath cycles, keeping the extended arm steady and the water motionless. Do this until you begin to feel an ache in your arm. Can you push through the ache?

4. Notice if the water begins to move as it gets harder to keep your arm up.

5. When your arm is too tired, bend your elbow slowly through several more breath cycles. Then try slowly lowering and raising your arm, keeping the water still.

6. Repeat this exercise with the other arm. Resist judgment regarding how long you're able to keep your arm raised.

It's Okay

Emotional freedom technique, or EFT, literally taps into meridian points used in Chinese medicine to reduce the body's arousal during emotional dysregulation. Use this tool to ground your body when your emotions become overpowering.

STEPS:

1. Start by tapping your left index and middle fingers on the outside of your right palm, under the pinky finger. As you tap, repeat the mantra "Even though my emotions are big, I'm okay."

2. Then with your left hand, tap the top of your nose where it meets your right eyebrow and repeat the same mantra.

3. From here, you will tap the far side of your right eyebrow, then under your eye, then under your nose, then under your chin, all with your left hand, repeating the mantra each time.

4. Tap the right side of your collarbone, then under your right armpit, and finally the top of your head, repeating your mantra each time.

5. When you finish, repeat the tapping sequence while inhaling through your nose and exhaling through pursed lips.

6. If you still feel agitated, try humming a short tune like "Twinkle, Twinkle, Little Star."

7. If you are still not as regulated as you would like, try counting by fours while breathing in through your nose and out through pursed lips, making your exhalation longer than your inhalation.

Focus on the Fist

This meditation exercise may seem simple but packs a lot of punch. It helps improve concentration and mindfulness while also doing double duty as a stress reducer.

STEPS:

1. At your desk or table, place the back of your hands on the surface and make a fist, fingers facing you, thumb over fingers.

2. Fix your gaze on the fingers on one hand and complete 2 mindful breath cycles.

3. On the next inhale, slowly extend your thumb as if it were a terribly difficult, very impressive feat.

4. As you exhale, extend your index finger the same way, keeping your gaze fixed.

5. Move through each finger on both hands this way, inhaling or exhaling with each extension.

6. After moving through all 10 fingers, reverse the process, bringing in each finger.

7. Repeat 5 times, keeping your gaze fixed on your fingers as you move them slowly with the breath. Notice small details about your hands as you breathe. If your mind wanders, gently invite it back to your hands and your deep breathing.

Mindful Stimming

Stimming, short for self-stimulation, is a common behavior for most folks but a more frequent habit for people with ADHD. This might look like chronic hair twisting, finger drumming, or knee bouncing, among other things. For most, it happens in a state of hyper-focus or boredom. Some people stim to manage anxiety or sensory overwhelm. There's nothing wrong with the need to stim, but bringing a mindfulness to the habit can help you understand why you stim, and if there's something else going on that needs addressing.

STEPS:

1. Take a few deep breaths and think about any chronic habits you have.

2. With your eyes closed, in a comfortable position, start the habitual behavior while moving through breath cycles.

3. Note any sensations that arise physically, mentally, or emotionally. Feelings that arise might be pleasurable or uncomfortable. Try not to judge either way.

4. Take a few more breaths, then open your eyes.

5. During your day, try to note when you stim. What was happening just before you began? Who were you with?

6. How does the stim make you feel in your body and mind?

7. Breathe through the feeling, positive or negative.

8. The goal is not to stop stimming or to judge the behavior, but simply to bring a mindfulness to it to allow you to set intentionality.

Blocked Breath

⚹ Relaxation Exercise　　　　　　　⏱ *5 minutes*

For some, restlessness can be physically unbearable, especially when you are restricted from moving as much as your body wishes. Use this exercise to help calm your body when that restless feeling takes over.

STEPS:

1. Wherever you are, inhale deeply, filling your lungs as much as you can. Imagine you are inhaling directly into the part of your body that most wants to move.

2. Holding the breath, tighten your abdomen and chest, squeezing like you're desperately trying to exhale but cannot, as if opposing forces are pushing upward against your diaphragm and downward in your throat, blocking the airway.

3. Do this until you must allow the air out. If you are in a place where you can make noise, exhale loudly.

4. Repeat as many times as you need to until you notice that the restlessness has subsided.

Fidget-Spinner Breathing

✻ *Concentration Exercise*   ◷ *5 minutes*

Some people find that using objects or body parts to occupy themselves can help them focus—they bounce or tap a knee, use a fidget spinner, tug an elastic band, or twirl a pen. But sometimes it is not appropriate to do so or can be distracting to others. Good news: we have a natural, built-in fidget aid that no one will notice if we use . . . our breath!

STEPS:

1. While standing or sitting, find an object to focus on for the next 5 minutes. Start making big, intentional breaths.

2. Play with your breath. First take some deep breaths, feeling the air as you inhale and listening to the sound as it leaves you.

3. Then take repeated shallow breaths.

4. Next, take clipped, staccato breaths, as if you are sniffing something quickly.

5. Continue to play with varying your breath in this way, being careful not to let it distract you from what you're meant to be attending to.

Generalizing tip: *If you notice that you're paying closer attention to your breath, bouncing knee, or fidget spinner, then it's not serving its purpose and has become a distraction. Let it go and try something else. You may need a break, a stretch, or a glass of water to redirect yourself.*

Be Nosy

At this point, you may be feeling slightly bored with paying attention to your breath. If you feel this way, acknowledge how you feel and practice not judging the boredom. This exercise is also an opportunity to change up your breathing a little.

STEPS:

1. Sit in a chair with your back straight and your shoulders back. Your eyes may be open or closed.

2. Press a finger against your left nostril to block it. Take a deep, slow breath into your right nostril as you count to 10.

3. Release your left nostril, block your right nostril, then exhale through your left nostril as you count to 10.

4. Repeat steps 2 and 3, but breathe through the left while blocking the right.

5. Repeat this cycle 20 times.

6. If you get the sequence wrong—into the right, out through the left; into the left, out through the right—go back to step 1 and start over until you can reach 20 breaths in the correct sequence.

Generalizing tip: Use this meditation to help calm yourself quickly when simple breathing doesn't seem to be working.

CHAPTER SIX

CALM *the* EMOTIONS

The meditations in this chapter focus on increasing self-compassion and your awareness of the connection of thoughts, behaviors, and emotions as a means of self-regulation. Many of these meditations are based on a combination of traditional Buddhist meditations and cognitive behavioral therapy.

STOP

If you have impulse control issues, one of the challenges to a mindfulness practice is *remembering* to be mindful so you have a chance to pause before reacting. Until this becomes second nature, you may need a little visual help, which we call "scaffolding," until you can do it on your own. For this exercise, you'll need tape, paper, and red and black markers, crayons, or pencils.

STEPS:

1. To prepare for this meditation, visualize a stop sign. Grab a pencil and a piece of scratch paper and jot down what the octagonal shape looks like.

2. Sit at a table with your paper and markers. Close your eyes and complete several mindful breath cycles. Visualize a large stop sign in your mind.

3. Open your eyes. As you continue your mindful breathing, begin to outline the stop sign.

4. Keep your attention on the task. Note how the marker sounds on the paper, how your fingers feel curled around the marker, how your body feels in the chair.

5. Outline the letters for the word *stop*, then color the interior of the sign red around the letters. Notice if any judgments about the way you draw enter your mind.

6. Draw several stop signs.

7. When you notice your mind wandering from the drawing task, use the acronym STOP.

   S—Stop coloring.

   T—Take a breath.

   O—Observe that your mind has wandered. Reorient to your intention.

   P—Proceed with your intention.

8. When you've finished coloring several signs, close your eyes and complete a few final mindful breath cycles.

9. Put your supplies away, noting how it feels to immediately clean up after a project.

10. Tape the signs around your house to use as visual reminders to use the STOP acronym before reacting. You may have to move the signs around occasionally so they don't disappear from your view.

Rate Your Mood

✲ *Mindfulness Exercise*   ⏱ *10 minutes*

Part of calming unruly emotions is being mindful of their intensity in certain triggering situations. This meditation helps you understand the size of your emotions by using a rating scale. By affixing a number to your emotions, you can track how their intensity fluctuates in response to certain triggers, as well as how your mindfulness practice may be helping steady big emotions.

EMOTIONS:

Afraid	Depleted	Powerless
Angry	Desperate	Rejected
Annoyed	Frustrated	Sad
Anxious	Grouchy	Shocked
Ashamed	Guilty	Vulnerable
Bored	Incapable	Worthless
Confused	Numb	

PHYSICAL SENSATIONS:

Achy	Heavy	Sore
Breathless	Hot	Suffocating
Buzzing	Itchy	Sweating
Cold	Jumpy	Tense
Dizzy	Nauseated	Throbbing
Empty	Numb	Tingling
Frozen	Shaking	

STEPS:

1. Get into a comfortable sitting position with your back straight and your eyes closed. Begin breathing mindfully and spend a few minutes focused only on your breath.

2. Shift your attention to the past week. Think of a situation in which you experienced intense negative emotions.

3. Breathing into this memory, look at the list of emotions and find ones associated with this situation.

4. Pick the biggest emotion and rate its intensity on a scale of 1 to 100, with 100 being the biggest possible feeling. Make a mental note of this number and move on.

5. Remember the situation and notice if your body tenses any-where. Look at the list of physical sensations and rate the intensity of the ones you feel on a scale of 1 to 100. Make a mental note of the numbers.

6. Breathe into that place in your body and release the tension.

7. If you can, remember another situation where your emotions were intense, and repeat steps 3 through 6.

8. Try this for up to five different memories, remembering to con-tinue your rhythmic breathing.

9. End your meditation with several mindful breaths.

Generalizing tip: *You may choose to write down the memories and their corresponding emotional and physical ratings. Keeping a log can help you become more mindful of triggers and patterns.*

Automatic Thoughts

We pass judgment automatically all day long. *That coffee tastes bitter. That flower is beautiful. That song is sad.* When we feel intense negative emotions, they're generally accompanied by automatic thoughts that are often similarly negative. An aim of cognitive therapy—and this meditation—is to bring an awareness to automatic thinking as the first step in reframing it.

STEPS:

1. In a comfortable position with your eyes open or closed, draw in several breaths, and release any tension as you exhale.

2. Consider a situation that led to an emotion rating over 60 on the intensity scale found in the previous meditation (page 66).

3. Read the following questions, then close your eyes and breathe as you meditate on their answers.

   What was I thinking as I felt this emotion?

   What am I afraid might happen?

   If that happens, what does it mean about me?

   What older memories or images relate to this situation?

4. Your answers are your automatic thoughts. Take note of them.

5. Of your automatic thoughts, is there one in particular that is stronger than the rest? This is called a "hot thought."

6. Breathe into your hot thought. Consider its connection to any older memories.

7. Take several more breaths and finish your meditation.

It's All Connected

⚶ *Mindfulness Exercise* ⏱ *10 minutes*

Our thoughts, emotions, behaviors, environment, and physical reactions are five areas of life that are so interconnected that a negative change in one can disrupt the entire system. This meditation will help you define the different facets of your experiences and become more mindful of this interconnection. You'll need to do the Rate Your Mood meditation (page 66) first.

STEPS:

1. From any comfortable position, close your eyes, and breathe deeply into your belly, following your breath in and out for several cycles.

2. When you're ready, think of a recent situation where you rated your emotions high on the scale (over 60).

3. Who were you with? Where and when did this happen?

4. Breathing through this visual, notice the negative thoughts that arise.

5. As a result of this situation and these emotions and thoughts, did you change your behavior?

6. Did any changes to your environment occur as a result of the chain reaction of your emotions, thoughts, and behaviors?

7. At the time, can you recall feeling any adverse physical sensations? Do you feel any now? If so, inhale into them and let them go on your exhale.

8. Finish this meditation with several minutes of mindful breathing, then open your eyes.

What's the Worst Thing That Could Happen?

✲ *Stress Management Exercise*   ⏲ *10 minutes*

Anxiety is often ADHD's best friend. And it's no wonder—missing parts of conversations, forgetting important dates, or being told you've done something wrong can make a person worry the worst will happen. This type of worrying in the extreme is called "catastrophic thinking." Cognitive behavioral therapy tackles catastrophic thinking with a series of Socratic questions that help you examine the reality of your fears. Use this meditation when anxiety and ADHD are ganging up on you.

STEPS:

1. In a comfortable position with your eyes open or closed, begin breathing mindfully and relax any tension in your body.

2. After several breaths, invite a worry into your mind. Notice whether physical tension accompanies it. Breathe into that feeling and try to release it.

3. Imagine the negative outcome if your worry happened. Breathe into that. Ask yourself why that outcome would be bad.

4. If that negative outcome happened, what would be the next negative outcome after it? And after that? Continue this process of questioning, breathing into each answer until you reach what you feel is a final answer.

5. Note how you feel with this final answer—sit with it, breathing into the feeling. On a scale of 1 to 100, what is the realistic percentage that this worst outcome will happen? Does your worry seem smaller or bigger as a result of this examination?

6. Give yourself a "reality check" by articulating why your worst fears are unlikely to come true. Here are some examples:

Worry: *I might not be able to focus enough to make this deadline.*

Negative outcome: *If I don't make the deadline, my boss will be mad.*

Next negative outcome: *If my boss is mad, they'll never promote me.*

Next negative outcome: *If I don't get promoted, I'll be stuck in this job forever.*

Worst outcome: *If I'm stuck here forever, I'll be miserable my whole life.*

Reality check: *Even if my boss is angry one time, I can make it up to them in other ways. I could probably still get promoted. Even if I'm not, there are other jobs. I don't have to be miserable forever.*

7. Breathe into that reality check, focusing on it for several breath cycles. During the day when you sense the same worry, try to bring that reality check into your awareness as needed, breathing through the emotion.

Mind Reader Challenge

⁂ *Cognitive Exercise* 🕐 *15 minutes*

I still recall the pit in my stomach after learning that three friends had lunch together without inviting me. *Maybe they don't like me. Or they forgot about me. Or they don't find me fun,* I thought. It turns out it had nothing to do with me. They'd simply bumped into each other and decided to share a meal. Assumptive leaps to thoughts of rejection are common for people with ADHD. This meditation can help us find peace and remind us that we're not mind readers.

STEPS:

1. Get into a comfortable position and begin breathing mindfully.

2. After several breaths, imagine you're out and you see a friend. You smile and wave, but they don't wave back; instead, they scowl.

3. With this visualization, note any sensations that come up. What's your immediate assumption about your friend's scowl?

4. How does this assumption make you feel emotionally? Do you tense up anywhere in your body? Does this assumption affect your behavior toward your friend? Breathe into the feeling and release it.

5. Picturing your friend's scowl, what's a second possible reason for their response? Repeat step 4.

6. Continue coming up with possibilities and repeating step 4. Can you think of any possible reasons that have nothing to do with you?

7. Note if step 4 feels different when you consider the reasons that have nothing to do with you.

8. When you're ready, imagine smiling at your friend with deep compassion for their scowl. Now imagine they smile back. Inhale, then exhale and open your eyes.

Generalizing tip: *The next time your gut assumes you're being rejected, consider doing this meditation to see if you can come up with other possibilities.*

Manage Your Mood

⚶ Emotional Regulation Exercise   ⏲ *20 minutes*

Now that you understand the interconnection of thoughts, behaviors, and emotions, and how certain triggers cause intense emotions, you can use this cognitive behavioral therapy–inspired meditation to help you manage this interconnection. You may find it helpful to have a pen and paper or a computer (with the internet turned off) to jot down thoughts that arise during this exercise.

STEPS:

1. Sit up straight and breathe deeply into your abdomen. As you exhale, release any tension from your body.

2. Take 5 mindful breaths, focusing on the feeling and sound of your breath.

3. Recall a recent challenging situation that resulted in an intense, negative mood. Rate the mood on a scale of 1 to 100, with 100 being the most intense.

4. What was going through your mind just before the intense emotion appeared? Ask yourself the questions from the Automatic Thoughts meditation (page 68). Write down your thoughts if you wish.

5. Considering your hot thought (the one thought that is stronger than the rest), meditate for several breath cycles on the evidence you use to support it. Write down this evidence if you wish.

6. On a scale of 1 to 100, with 100 being the most realistic, how realistic is this evidence?

7. Can you consider contrary evidence to support an alternate, more balanced thought? If you wish, write down this evidence.

8. Keeping this more balanced possibility in mind, take several mindful breaths into your abdomen, relaxing any physical tension.

9. Now re-rate the same mood you rated in step 3. Has the number decreased now that you've weighed the alternatives? Consider any changes without judgment.

10. Complete several more breath cycles and continue with your day.

Generalizing tip: Using this type of thought record to track your moods over time can be a powerful way to increase your ability to be aware of, examine, and then manage the intensity of your feelings.

A Balancing Act

This exercise delves further into common types of cognitive distortions that can take hold of our thinking and steer us in unhelpful directions. The following is a list of cognitive distortions and examples. Use this meditation to balance the extreme of these thought patterns with more balanced approaches.

All-or-nothing thinking: *If I don't finish this section by 9 a.m., I might as well quit the whole thing.*

Overgeneralization: *My boss didn't like my idea. They hate everything I do.*

Filtering: *Everyone seemed to like my presentation, but John said he couldn't hear me well. I blew it.*

Discounting: *Everyone seemed to like my presentation. They must have been in a good mood because the presenter before me was funny.*

Catastrophizing: *The presentation didn't go as planned. I'll never be able to pull off a presentation on my own.*

Personalization: *I wasn't asked to join the meeting. It's because they didn't like my presentation.*

Should: *John said he couldn't hear my presentation well. I should learn to enunciate and talk louder.*

Labeling: *My boss had some criticism about my presentation. I'm such a failure.*

Blame: *The presentation didn't go as I planned. If only my coworker had had a chance to review it. It's all their fault.*

STEPS:

1. Determine one or two cognitive distortions that you may be succumbing to.

2. Ground yourself in a basic meditation, breathing mindfully.

3. After several breath cycles, visualize an empty balancing scale.

4. Place your unhelpful thought on one side of the scale.

   The presentation didn't go as planned. I'll never be able to pull off a presentation on my own.

5. What thought could you place on the other side to bring a balance to it?

   That was the first presentation I've ever done. It takes practice. The next one will be easier.

6. Visualize the scale equalizing, bringing a balance to your thoughts. Breathe into this balance.

7. Place your next unhelpful thought on the scale and repeat steps 5 and 6.

8. When you finish balancing your thoughts, conclude with 3 mindful breath cycles.

What's Your Name?

✳ *Emotional Regulation Exercise*   ⏱ *5 minutes*

Narrative psychotherapy uses something called "externalizing" to remind us we're not the problem—the problem is the problem. This is done by naming the problem and talking to and about the problem as if it were something external from you. This helps when you feel that big emotions and struggles with executive functioning seem to define who you are.

STEPS:

1. Sit with your back straight, eyes closed, and hands folded in your lap.

2. Inhale, and as you exhale, relax into your body. Notice only your breath. Repeat this three times.

3. As you settle into meditation, focus on a negative feeling that has been weighing you down, such as anxiety or impulsivity.

4. Identify this feeling and acknowledge its presence. For instance, you could say, *Anxiety is here right now*.

5. Take 3 deep breaths to breathe into this acknowledgment. Visualize this named struggle as a form, like a dragon, cloud, or other thing. How does this problem get in your way?

6. Take 3 more deep breaths. This time, as you inhale, imagine stepping away from the "thing". As you exhale, tell the form, *You are not me*.

7. Notice any feelings that arise as you separate from this problem.

8. Continue mindful breath cycles until you're ready to open your eyes.

Two Truths and a Lie

✳ *Compassion Exercise*　　　　　　　　⏱ *5 minutes*

We often follow compliments given to us with an explanation of why we aren't deserving.

Friend: *The sweater you knit is so good. I love the cabling.*

Us: *Yes, but it took me forever.*

This diminishes our accomplishment and reinforces our lack of self-worth. Use this meditation to examine the ways you diminish yourself so you can move toward openly accepting another's appreciation.

STEPS:

1. Settle into a comfortable position. Complete 3 mindful breath cycles.

2. Try to recall the last compliment you received. If you're unable to, then imagine someone complimenting you for a task you're currently working on.

3. Notice any feelings that arise from this compliment. Are you able to accept the compliment without discomfort?

4. Notice if you feel the urge to discount the compliment.

5. Imagine yourself simply thanking the person for their kind words. Notice what sensations arise from this simple acceptance.

6. Breathe into these sensations and end your meditation.

Generalizing tip: *The next time you're complimented, be mindful of your physical and emotional responses. Don't discount it; simply say, "Thank you."*

When You Were a Child

⚘ *Compassion Exercise*   ⏱ *20 minutes*

Our sense of self develops primarily from our early experiences. Unfortunately, for children with ADHD, many of those experiences involved negative feedback. This meditation is an opportunity to offer compassion and encouragement to your child-self, as a step to offering it to your present self. It's best done with a pen and paper or on a computer (with the internet turned off). If you prefer, you can have an imaginary conversation with your child-self instead.

STEPS:

1. Get into a comfortable position, relax your body, close your eyes, and draw in a few deep, mindful breaths.

2. When you're ready, recall a particularly difficult time from your childhood, particularly one that relates to your executive functioning struggles.

3. Notice what comes up mentally, emotionally, or physically, and breathe into that feeling, letting it go as you exhale.

4. Begin writing a letter to (or having a conversation with) yourself in the third person (e.g., *Dear Merriam*).

5. Acknowledge the difficult time this child is having. Let this child know they're seen by you and that you feel great compassion for them.

6. Describe, without judgment, the feelings this child is having.

7. Offer words of encouragement, like you might to a friend or child who is struggling now. What do you wish someone had said to you at the time?

8. When you finish, close your eyes and imagine hugging the child tightly, offering them love.

9. Sit with this image, breathing through it for several breaths until you're ready to open your eyes.

Generalizing tip: *This is a great exercise to do as part of regular journaling. You can switch it up by writing a letter to your present self from your future self for times when you are struggling.*

Compassion with a Twist

★ *Compassion Exercise*   ⏱ *20 minutes*

A traditional compassion meditation acknowledges general suffering as a part of life and gives permission to the self to feel compassion for this suffering. Feeling compassion creates oxytocin in the brain, which helps in your journey to improve your relationships and overall well-being. This meditation puts a slight spin on it; instead of focusing on general "suffering," you'll acknowledge that executive functioning challenges are a part of your life and that you deserve compassion for these challenges that you never asked for.

STEPS:

1. Get into a comfortable position, close your eyes, and take a few mindful breaths.

2. Think about an executive functioning challenge that you believe may contribute to any feelings of low self-worth. What strategy could counter this challenge? Here are some examples of challenges and their countering healthy strategies.

CHALLENGE		HEALTHY STRATEGY
Unmotivated	▸	Set intentions before tasks
Disorganized	▸	Be mindful of putting things in their place
Forgetful	▸	Check calendars often and use alarm reminders
Easily distracted	▸	Use breaks and the Pomodoro Technique (page 27) to stay on task
Impulsive	▸	Use the STOP visual (page 64) to pause and make mindful choices
Restless	▸	Access breath and body relaxation strategies to calm down
Easily angered	▸	Notice physical tension and breathe through it to calm down

3. Find a touch that feels soothing and comforting—for example, place your hand on your heart or abdomen, wrap your arms around your shoulders, or hold your face.

4. Think of your challenge, playing it out in your mind.

5. As you think on your challenge, repeat these words to yourself: *This challenge is a moment of suffering and is a part of my life. It's okay to be kind to myself. I need compassion just like other people do. I'm trying.*

6. Repeat this mantra through several breath cycles.

7. Then, through several more breath cycles, repeat a mantra that's the strategy to overcome your challenge, such as *I'm trying to be one who sets intentions before tasks. I'm trying to be one who uses breaks. May I be filled with self-compassion as I try.*

8. Finish by directing as much warm compassion and loving-kindness to yourself as you can. Then, have a great day!

Bon Voyage, Inner Critic!

⚬ *Compassion Exercise*   ⏱ *10 minutes*

The ADHD monkey mind doubles as an inner critic. An inner critic may feel like a bully sometimes, but it's often our minds' misguided attempt to protect us by keeping us on high alert. When our inner critics chastise us for a mistake, they do so in the hopes that we won't make that mistake again. But instead of receiving the criticism as a cautionary lesson, we typically internalize this self-talk and conclude that we're bad, a failure, or not smart. This meditation will invite your inner critic to take a vacation from the job you never asked it to do.

STEPS:

1. Prime yourself for this visual exercise by getting into a comfortable position. Close your eyes. Breathe into any physically tense areas and release.

2. After a few mindful breaths, imagine the last thing you felt you did wrong because of your ADHD. Did you forget an appointment, lose something important, or blurt out something insensitive? How did you feel about yourself as a result?

3. Imagine the event is a movie and the resulting feeling is a critic reviewing that movie. This critic thinks their role is to help point out errors so that next time you'll do better.

4. Thank your critic for doing an excellent job. Let them know that although they're trying to protect you from making the same mistake again, they're not achieving their goal and are only making you feel bad.

5. Tell your critic to take a vacation. Visualize your critic packing a bag and getting on an airplane, waving goodbye.

6. Inhale deeply and, as you exhale, visualize the plane taking off.

7. Once your inner critic has taken flight, invite a new helper to take the vacant job—the "inner compassionater." Their job is to remind you that you deserve self-compassion and ensure that the inner critic stays on vacation.

8. Picture your inner compassionater arriving and unpacking their suitcase to move in permanently.

9. Recall a time when you felt nurtured, warm, and cozy. Recognize that this inner compassionater embodies an unconditional love for you and makes you feel that same warmth.

10. Breathe into the feeling of deep, warm compassion for yourself.

11. Repeat silently or aloud, *I am loved, and I love myself. I deserve this love, and I deserve compassion.*

12. Breathe into the compassion. Notice if the inner critic tries to book a return flight. Visualize your inner compassionater blocking the door, then wrapping their arms around you, flooding you with compassion.

13. Sit with this warm feeling, breathing it into your belly for several breath cycles. On an exhale, open your eyes fully.

Double Breathing

☆ Stress Reduction Exercise ○ *5 minutes*

Picture a little child whose ice cream has just toppled onto the sidewalk. They're sobbing so much that they can't catch their breath. They double inhale—two short inhalations followed by an exhale. This "double breathing" is the body's natural reaction to intense stress and is called a physiological sigh. During stress, the tiny sacs in the lungs deflate, making it harder to expel the buildup of carbon dioxide. Physiological sighs reinflate the sacs so we can get rid of carbon dioxide and replace it with the necessary oxygen. Several double breaths in a row can be the quickest route to calming the body down. The next time big emotions take hold of you, try this double breathing meditation to regain control of your body and mind.

STEPS:

1. In a moment when you're overwhelmed and regular deep breathing isn't helping, purposefully draw in a shallow, half breath and then pause for 2 seconds.

2. Instead of exhaling that shallow breath, immediately follow it with another shallow breath in.

3. After the second shallow breath in, exhale slowly.

4. Repeat this several times and then follow with as many deep, slow, mindful breaths as you need until you feel calm.

Motivational Interviewing

✻ *Emotional Regulation Exercise*   ⏲ *20 minutes*

Sometimes we get stuck repeating dysfunctional behaviors, even when we know better. Maybe we're ambivalent about setting calendar reminders, even though we know we'll forget appointments if we don't; or, we refuse to stick to a routine, even though we know life would function more easily. Motivational interviewing helps promote behavior change by exploring conflicting feelings with acceptance and compassion. This meditation can help you use the same technique on your own.

STEPS:

1. Sit with your back straight and tall and your eyes closed. Begin breathing mindfully.

2. As you breathe, consider the behavior you're ambivalent about changing. You know it would be good for you to change, but you can't seem to get yourself to do it.

3. Breathe into the image of this behavior without judging yourself.

4. Repeat to yourself, *I have the resources within me to change in this way, if I so choose.*

5. Now imagine this behavior as something separate from yourself. See yourself coming up alongside it. You're not fighting against it. You're simply looking at it.

6. Imagine there's something between you and this behavior that's blocking you from it. What stops you from this behavior?

7. Note this resistance and any sensation that arises. Breathe into it.

CONTINUED

8. Are there any positives to your life as a result of not changing this behavior?

9. Breathe into this thought.

10. Are there any negatives that result from not changing?

11. If you were to remove this block and change the behavior, what good would come of it?

12. Breathe into the visual of this good, noticing any feelings that arise.

13. Are there any negatives that arise from making this change? Breathe through them.

14. Before ending your meditation, repeat, *I have the resources within me to change in this way, if I so choose*—and breathe.

Generalizing tip: *This type of meditation may not change your ambivalence in one sitting. A frequent gentle inquiry into the positives and negatives of behavior change may be necessary before you begin to see a shift in one direction.*

CHAPTER SEVEN

MORNING

When I was younger, I dreaded the morning. I never got enough sleep, I was always rushed to get out the door, and my body and mind felt resentful that they were being prematurely forced into the sun. Mindfulness has given me a new appreciation for the morning. Now I relish it for its quiet and the opportunity to reflect on the day ahead. The meditations in this chapter focus on deepening your mindfulness practice to help get you started on the right foot so your day can be an intentional one.

Rise and Shine

⚘ Mindfulness Exercise   ⏲ *5 to 10 minutes*

If you're not a morning person, waking up can be brutal. You mindlessly shuffle to the coffee pot, completely unaware of how you even got there as you take your first sip. This meditation can help clear that morning fog from your brain before you even take a step so you can move through your day with greater intentionality.

STEPS:

1. Before you lift your head off of the pillow, take a deep breath. Imagine breathing in the energy of a new day.

2. As you breathe out, visualize your exhale blowing away the fog from your brain.

3. Check in with your body. Breathe into aches and tension, and relax as you breathe out.

4. Without hesitation, swing your legs over the side of the bed. Keep your eyes open to allow the natural morning light to assist in waking you.

5. On an inhale, straighten your spine and pull your shoulders back like you are trying to touch the bottom of your shoulder blades together. Hold this squeeze for a breath and release.

6. On your next breath, feel the ground under your feet. Is it soft or hard? Chilly or warm?

7. Check in with your body in this position. Are you cold or hot? Achy anywhere?

8. Open your eyelids wide. Smile on the next breath cycle, stretching your cheeks wide.

9. Check in on your mind, without judgment. Are you feeling groggy or refreshed? Who and what is on your mind? Are you pressed for time?

10. On your next breath, set an intention for the next hour—something like, *I'm going to make time to play with the kids before school,* or *I will eat breakfast sitting down while I read the paper.*

11. Take a mindful breath and rise with an intention for the kind of day you want to have.

Macro and Micro Intentions

✻ *Mindfulness Exercise* ○ *5 minutes*

Sometimes it can feel like life itself is two steps ahead of us, as our brains constantly play catchup. *What did that person just say? Where am I supposed to be right now? Why did I come into this room?* Our minds are either going a mile a minute or completely asleep at the wheel! Strengthening your mindfulness muscles can help combat this feeling as you progress through your day with awareness of the present moment. One way to help make those mindful muscles strong is to set intentions for how you want to be during your day, both on a micro and macro level. For this meditation, you'll need an alarm or other device that can notify you throughout the day.

STEPS:

1. At the end of your morning meditation, finish by setting at least one big picture, or macro, intention for your state of being, something you wish to embody throughout the day. Here are some examples:

    Today, I will be a good listener.

    Today, I will slow down as I do my tasks.

    Today, I will take breaks every 20 minutes to stand and stretch.

2. Next, go to your alarm or notification device. Set at least three alarms for different times throughout the day.

3. When the alarm sounds, if you can, stop what you're doing and complete up to 3 slow breath cycles. During your breathing, bring awareness to the intention you set. Don't judge whether

you've been successful keeping your intention. This is an opportunity to reset, if necessary, or simply enjoy a moment of mindfulness.

4. During the day, set micro intentions for smaller tasks before you begin a project or a meeting or a conversation. Here are some examples:

Before I write this chapter, I'll turn off the internet and practice the Pomodoro Technique (page 27) to keep track of distracting thoughts.

I'll use breath as a fidget aid during this meeting so I can pay attention to the boss when she makes her presentation.

I'll keep my brain and body engaged in the conversation I'm about to have with my mother.

5. Set alarm notifications for your micro intentions if you need to.

Generalizing tip: *You can practice setting intentions with any of your meditations. Your intention can be the stated goal of the meditation, or you can set your intention to be aware of the sounds around you, your breath, or your body. Then set alarms for every 3 minutes to help bring you back to that intention in case your mind has wandered.*

What's Your Routine?

Many people do the same thing every morning to get ready for their day. And they're often rushed as they get ready, to the extent that they stop thinking about what they're doing. This exercise will help develop a general mindfulness of changing from one step to the next—and the reasons why—during your morning routine.

STEPS:

1. Before getting out of bed, take 3 deep, mindful breaths, paying attention to the air as it enters and exits. Release any physical tension and open your eyes wide to welcome the morning light.

2. Swing your legs over the side of the bed, and as you complete a breath cycle, set an intention for your morning: *I'm going to notice each step as I get ready for work.*

3. Stand, and as you start your routine, narrate your movements.

   I'm going downstairs for coffee.

   I'm waking up the kids.

   I'm turning on the water for a shower.

4. Tell yourself why you're taking this step.

   I can't wake up without coffee.

   The kids slept through their alarm.

   A shower helps me wake up first thing.

5. As you complete the step, notice any physical, mental, or emotional sensations, especially ones that may be different from before you started the step. Is the coffee bitter? Are you frustrated because the children won't wake up? Does the hot water feel so good you don't want to turn off the shower?

6. Simply notice. Try not to judge. Remember to breathe.

7. Repeat steps 3 through 6 for each part of your morning routine.

Mindful Morning Munching

  ✦ *Mindfulness Exercise*　　　　　　　① *20 minutes*

A common approach to developing mindfulness is noticing what you eat. For this exercise, many people suggest a raisin, as the idea is to hone your focus using something small. Since the morning rush is often chaotic for people with ADHD, breakfast is frequently the first thing to get cut. But studies have shown that protein can improve our ability to focus, so I recommend building 20 minutes into your schedule to mindfully eat a protein-filled breakfast.

STEPS:

1. Sit down in front of your healthy, delicious meal. With your back straight, place your hands softly on the table.

2. Inhale, and as you do, express gratitude for the food you're about to eat.

3. As you lift the food to your mouth, notice how it feels in your hand. Is the utensil cold? Look at the food. Is it rough or soft?

4. Exhale before you take a bite.

5. Take a reasonably sized bite of food. Notice its temperature, its texture, its flavor. Notice if it is sweet or salty. Does it taste as you expected it to?

6. Chew the food more slowly than normal. Then chew more quickly than normal, noting any difference in sensations.

7. As you swallow, note the feeling as the food moves down your throat and into your stomach.

8. Before you take another bite, complete a full, deep breath cycle.

9. Chew your next bite 30 times or until it loses texture.

10. Next, take a small bite of food and resist the immediate urge to chew.

11. Roll it around your tongue and notice its texture before you begin chewing.

12. For each bite and drink of this meal, try to keep a mindful awareness of what you're consuming. If your mind wanders from the food, gently return to it until you're full and finished eating.

13. Before rising from the table, complete 3 breath cycles with your back straight and your eyes closed, expressing gratitude for the food.

Generalizing tip: Of course, this meditation can be done anytime you eat. Mindfully cleaning your dishes after your breakfast will not only further your practice but also help reduce cleanup later.

What If You Start Your Day This Way?

✳ *Emotional Regulation Exercise*   ◷ *20 minutes*

What if you were able to turn negative thoughts about yourself upside down? What if you could challenge them, examine their merit, and redefine them? This series of what-if questions helps you meditate on the narrative you and others tell you about yourself and examines whether it's helping or hurting you.

STEPS:

1. Sitting with your back straight and your feet firmly planted on the ground, close your eyes and inhale. Breathe into the bottom of your belly, focusing your attention on your body, feeling gravity's tug. Breathe in loving-kindness. Breathe out any tension.

2. After several moments of mindful breathing, open your eyes and ponder the following questions:

   What if everything I was told about myself when I was little was wrong?

   What if I found out that my school environment was not ideal for how I learned?

   What if I'm smarter than I've been led to believe?

   What if I'm more capable than teachers, parents, and friends gave me credit for?

   What if I were able to forgive them?

   What if I stopped identifying with the negative feedback from my past?

   What if I acknowledged that I'm a creative being with an amazing mind?

What if I accepted that if I spent time engaging in a mindfulness practice, I could exert more control over my awareness?

What if I were able to tap into that awareness and, without judgment, fully experience this present moment?

What would that mean for my life, for my relationships, and for work?

3. Breathe between each question, imagining the breath traveling all the way to your feet and then into the earth below. There's no need to come up with answers and no need to judge feelings that arise. Simply notice what comes up and breathe into it.

4. When you finish the questions, close your eyes and spend the remaining time focused on your breath.

5. When you're ready, take a deep breath and open your eyes.

Generalizing tip: Answers to these questions may pop into your mind throughout the day. Some days you might find yourself experiencing a sadness and loss because of your answers. Other days you might feel angry or be overwhelmingly inspired. Anything you feel is natural and normal. Notice it without judgment. And remember to breathe.

Morning Showers

※ Mindfulness Exercise ⏱ *10 minutes*

The shower is a wonderful place to practice mindfulness; however, it's usually a time when we complete routine steps on autopilot as our minds wander. Since you're stuck until you finish, you might as well use the opportunity to strengthen your moment-to-moment awareness. Your time in the shower can be used to cleanse your body as well as your monkey mind!

STEPS:

1. Before you turn on the water, inhale and bring your awareness to your breath.

2. As you place your hand on the knobs to turn on the water, note the temperature of the knobs and how they feel on your skin.

3. See the water as it spills from the shower head. Follow it down to where it splashes and runs down the drain. Note the sound the water makes.

4. Reach into the water with your hand. How does it feel? Is the pressure high or low? Is the water too hot, too cold, or just right?

5. Before you step in, take note of your breath.

6. As you enter the shower, keep your mind on the feel of the water as it tumbles over you. Was there a slight shock at first before your body got used to the feeling? How does your body respond to being in water?

7. Notice if you stand motionless for a moment or if you dive immediately into washing.

8. As you start your cleansing routine, bring an awareness to new physical sensations, from the feel of the shampoo bottle in your hand to the soap being lathered on your skin.

9. Move slightly slower than normal, giving your mind time to acknowledge your body's actions.

10. As you wash, keep your attention on the feel of your hands on your skin.

11. When you finish, turn the water off and stay present, noting the temperature change. Are you immediately cold? Do you rush to the towel? How does the towel feel?

12. Note the bathroom as you step out of the shower stall. Is it warm and filled with steam? Is it quiet?

13. As you dry yourself off, notice if your mind wanders from the action and gently bring it back. Try to stay with this mindfulness until you leave the bathroom.

Journaling the Morning Monkey Mind

⁂ Mindfulness Exercise　　　　　⏱ *10 minutes*

The process of regular journaling has been shown in numerous clinical trials to decrease anxiety and depression and increase an overall sense of well-being. Morning journaling can be a great way to set intentions as well as a forum for your monkey mind to swing freely from tree to tree without restraint. By setting a morning routine of journaling, you signal to your mind that it will have a contained place in which you'll pay attention to its worries, fears, and wacky ideas, and then it will be time to move on with intentionality. A recent study from researchers at the University of Tokyo indicates that the use of pen and paper positively increases brain activity, especially in the area of improved memory, so for this exercise I suggest a paper journal.

STEPS:

1. In a comfortable position with your back straight and a journal and a pen accessible, close your eyes and complete several mindful breath cycles.

2. While breathing, visualize the monkeys in your mind, swinging from tree to tree. Let them know that for the next 20 minutes, they're invited to screech and holler and play to their hearts' content, but after that, you request quiet for the rest of the day.

3. Before writing, check in with your emotions and body. On a scale of 1 to 10, with 10 being the best, rate how you feel in both categories. Write these numbers on the first line. Keeping numeric track of your feelings can help you become mindful of how they might be influenced.

4. Begin writing whatever comes to mind. Feel free to write concerns, big emotions, happy plans, terrible ideas, or angry thoughts.

5. If you can't think of what to write, then write, *I can't think of what to write, so I'm going to write about what my five senses notice in this moment.* Then write about that until your monkey mind comes up with something else.

6. Write for the prescribed amount of time. Upon finishing, close your eyes and imagine the day ahead of you. Set your intention for the day and its goals. It might be something like this: *Today I'll be kind to myself and remember to smile. I'll write two chapters, work out for 30 minutes, meditate for 10 minutes, have lunch with Sally and listen mindfully, and read instead of watching TV before bed.*

7. As you close the cover of your journal, take in a deep breath. Remind the monkeys that play time is over. If they make noise later, gently invite them to wait until tomorrow morning's journaling session to voice their concerns.

Every Day, in Every Way, I'm Feeling . . .

☆ *Mantra Exercise*   ⏱ *5 minutes*

There's a physiological reason that mantras tend to work. Repeating a phrase over and over forces you to focus on the thought or feeling that accompanies it. And by focusing on a new, more positive thought, you're actively using a new neural pathway. The pathway gets stronger the more it's used, making it easier for the brain to choose that path as an alternative to your old, well-trodden negative road. Dr. Émile Coué realized this long before brain scan technology was available when, in his 1920 book *Self Mastery through Conscious Autosuggestion*, he suggested his patients repeat the mantra "Every day, in every way, I'm getting better and better." For this meditation, feel free to use Dr. Coué's mantra, or create one of your own. Here are some examples:

Every day, in every way, I'm feeling more . . .

. . . motivated and focused.

. . . organized and attentive.

. . . compassionate and driven.

. . . calm and productive.

STEPS:

1. If you're creating your own mantra, I suggest making a list of positive words and taping it someplace where you'll see it—where you work or meditate, on the bathroom mirror, or on the refrigerator.

2. Each day, pick two new words and repeat your mantra as many times a day as you can remember for at least 30 seconds each time. The longer you repeat the mantra, the more your brain will strengthen that neural pathway.

3. The moments you take to repeat your mantra are also opportunities to breathe mindfully and check in with your body.

4. As you say the mantra, visualize yourself embodying these new words with conviction.

Clean Up Your Act

Clutter can be a bit of an issue. Dirty dishes, clothes strewn about, piles of paper—tidying up generally isn't a strength of someone with ADHD. I'll often let things pile up, and then when I have a moment, I'll pop in an audiobook to try to distract myself so I don't notice that I'm cleaning. But cleaning time can also be good for practicing mindfulness. When you're cleaning up, instead of grumbling about it, use this moment to exercise self-care and deepen your practice. Starting the morning with a clean and de-cluttered space can help your mind feel similarly de-cluttered as you progress through the day.

STEPS:

1. When you decide to collect the cleaning supplies, feel yourself move to their location. Listen to any sounds. Do your clothes rustle? Do your shoes click on the floor? If you're barefoot, feel the bottom of your feet on the ground.

2. Feel your hand as it curls around the broom handle, rag, or bottle of cleaner. If you're de-cluttering, feel the texture of whatever object you're putting away.

3. Notice your breath, if it's fast or slow, deep or shallow.

4. These tasks can be a bit boring, so as you clean, narrate to yourself what you're doing:

   I am wiping down the counter. The cloth is wet and feels cool on my hand.

   I am folding my sweater. It feels soft, and the wool is thick.

I am moving this dish to the dishwasher. It's a blue plate and has a chip on the edge.

5. Your mind will wander from the cleaning. You may find it tiresome. You may wonder why you can't keep anything clean. You may feel frustrated. That's okay. Notice your feelings, take a breath, and continue narrating your actions.

6. As you clean, remember to check in with your physical sensations and remember your breath.

7. Once you're finished, put away your supplies. Go to the center of the room you cleaned and take a mindful breath with your eyes closed.

8. Open your eyes and take in the newly cleaned and organized room. Note how the sense of order feels. As you go through the day, remind yourself of that feeling whenever you tackle tasks requiring organization.

Metta in the Morning

꙳ *Compassion Exercise*   ⏱ *5 minutes*

Metta meditation is a practice of fostering loving-kindness for yourself and others. After a lifetime of being told to do things better, quiet down, try harder, be more organized, and pay attention, it can be easy not to feel loving-kindness for yourself and instead feel undeserving of it. Use this simple meditation when you feel a bit low to get your day off to a better start.

STEPS:

1. With your eyes closed, picture yourself in a situation where ADHD usually gets in the way.

2. Complete several breath cycles, remaining focused on this visual. Acknowledge that you desire love and kindness and that it's okay to wish this, even though you might not always feel worthy. Acknowledge that you deserve this love and kindness, as do all people.

3. Breathe through any negative self-talk that appears.

4. On your next inhale, keeping your visual in mind, repeat the classic metta mantra: *May I be filled with loving-kindness. May I be well. May I be peaceful and at ease. May I be happy.*

5. Continue repeating the mantra with the rhythm of your breath, allowing your heart to be genuinely open to this sentiment.

6. Breathe in loving-kindness for yourself, and breathe out feelings that you're unworthy of this self-love.

Generalizing tip: Feel free to substitute the positive mantra with one specific to ADHD, such as May I be filled with focus and calm. May I be safe from impulsive risk-taking. May I acknowledge my own efforts.

CHAPTER EIGHT

EVENING

Evenings often come with a host of transitions—such as work to home, dinner to sleep, and bustling interaction to quiet alone time. Transitions can sometimes be jarring, but these are great opportunities for mindfulness. The meditations in this chapter aim to help you stay mindful during your interactions, transitions, and daily reflections as you unwind and prepare for dreamland.

The Doorknob

Coming home from work, or from picking up the kids at school, can be stressful. It's a change from whatever you were doing or thinking about the moment before. You may suddenly be thrown into a stimulating environment with excited family members, filled with questions and demands and big emotions. You might feel as though you left your brain back on the bus, and it hasn't joined you just yet. This mindfulness exercise can help you transition into the situation that awaits inside your home.

STEPS:

1. Before you enter your home, pause with your hand on the doorknob. Don't open the door.

2. Close your eyes and complete up to 3 mindful breath cycles.

3. Repeat to yourself: *I am entering the house.*

4. What do you want to leave behind? Check in with residual feelings that have nothing to do with what awaits you inside.

5. Breathe and let those feelings float away.

6. What's inside? Excited children? A messy space? Too much quiet or too much stimulation?

7. Breathe into this expectation; welcome it and make room for it.

8. What do you want to bring inside with you? Carry forth the mindfulness of this moment as you hold on to the doorknob.

9. Set your intention for how you want to be. Take in one more mindful breath and on your exhale, open the door.

Instant Replay

⁎ Memory Exercise   ⏱ *15 minutes*

Morning is a great time to set intentions, and evening is the perfect time to review them. I like this meditation because it not only brings an awareness to your goals; it reinforces them, and also helps build memory skills. This meditation can be done formally or as you lie in bed and wind down to go to sleep.

STEPS:

1. Begin breathing mindfully, releasing tension from any stiff areas.

2. In reverse chronological order, replay your day. Visualize what you were doing before you got into bed or into your meditation position.

3. Go back to what you were doing before that, and then before that. Continue going backward until you arrive at the moment you opened your eyes to start your day.

4. Were you able to be mindful in the scenes of your day? If you set an intention for yourself, were you able to carry it forth? Try not to judge either way.

5. If you're in bed, you may drift to sleep before you play through your entire day. That's fine. Try again tomorrow night!

Generalizing tip: *If your mind gets lost in the replay of a certain scene and wanders down a rabbit hole, return to the scene and move on to the next one.*

Do-Over

This can be a companion exercise to the previous one, especially if you're stuck on a certain scene from your day. It's a good way to review your intentions, exercise mindfulness, and develop a greater understanding of difficult moments. Use this exercise to review your triggers and responses during heated scenes or even during a simple trip to the grocery store.

STEPS:

1. From a comfortable position or as a continuation of the Instant Replay meditation (page 115), inhale deeply into your abdomen, keeping your awareness on the sound and feel of your breath.

2. Release your breath slowly and, with it, release any tension from your body.

3. Complete several more breath cycles, and when you're ready, pick an event that happened during the day. It could be a household chore, a task at work, or an emotional interchange with a family member.

4. Think about how the event started. What were you doing just before that?

5. If the event resulted in intense feelings, can you pinpoint what set them off?

6. If the event was emotionless, how present were you in the moment?

7. Consider whether your intentions were reflected in your actions.

8. Could you have said, done, or thought something differently so the situation would have a different outcome, however small?

9. Notice feelings, thoughts, or sensations that arise while you're considering this scene.

10. Replay the scene in your mind, changing the action to change the outcome.

11. After replaying the scene, check in with your present thoughts, feelings, or sensations and notice if they've changed from a few minutes ago.

12. When you're ready, take several breaths and release the past, resetting your intentions for tomorrow, if necessary.

I'm Listening! I'm Listening!

✳ *Mindfulness Exercise* ⏱ *5 to 20 minutes*

Human connection sustains us. It generates the release of hormones like oxytocin to regulate stress and promote trust and love. Studies have shown that connection is as important for survival as food and sleep. Given that communication is integral to connection, one might imagine humans would be highly skilled at listening and expressing, but, in general, we're not! Active listening requires an ability to set aside one's thoughts and emotions and take in a contextual understanding of the words being spoken. For those with ADHD, this can be an added challenge, as paying attention to another person requires dopamine that may not be present. Fortunately, active listening is a skill that can be developed and can markedly improve the quality of relationships. Use this exercise with friends and loved ones to download the day's events and truly soak them in. You may notice that with daily practice, you'll deepen your ability to listen and strengthen your relationships.

STEPS:

1. Before you enter into the conversation, set your intention while drawing in a deep breath: *I will be present and truly listen.*

2. Start listening actively by facing the person speaking, keeping your eyes set comfortably in their direction.

3. Check in with your facial expressions. Use nonverbal gestures, such as smiles and nods, or simple acknowledgments, such as, "Uh-huh," and "Really?" to cue that you're listening.

4. Notice the other person's facial expression and the inflections in their tone. Can you assume their emotions based on these two things?

5. Take in the words the speaker is saying. Let them finish talking. Release any judgments you may be forming about them.

6. Notice any urge to respond with your own thoughts, experiences, or counterpoints. Pause and resist that urge.

7. Use questions, statements, clarifications, and summaries with your conversation partner to reflect what you've heard. This is reflective listening. It helps clarify your understanding of what's being said and helps your conversation partner feel heard.

   Them: *I kept trying to defend myself in the meeting, but my boss continually cut me off. I didn't know what to do.*

   Your options:

   That's really frustrating. **(emotion reflection)**

   Were you frustrated? **(question)**

   You didn't know what to do. **(statement)**

   Sounds like it may have been frustrating. **(clarification)**

   You kept trying to say something, but he wouldn't let you. Wow. **(summary)**

8. If the person talks for so long that your mind wanders, gently return to the conversation once you notice your attention has drifted. You may need to ask them to repeat themselves. Saying

CONTINUED

"I'm sorry, could you repeat that?" is often a much easier fix than trying to put clues together about what you may have missed; this creates anxiety that blocks you from further active and reflective listening.

9. Active listening can be especially useful for rejection sensitivity. Notice any rejection-like emotions during the conversation. Instead of leaping to conclusions, pause and breathe into the feeling. Ask for more information.

   Them: *I don't think you should come to the dinner with Mary.*

   You (assuming you're not wanted, maybe Mary doesn't like you): *So you'd rather I not come. I don't want to take that personally, but it's a little challenging. Could you clarify?*

   Them: *Oh, Mary is going through a rough divorce. She asked me to dinner for some free legal advice. It's not going to be a fun night.*

10. When the conversation ends, take a moment to reflect on it. How did using active listening change the experience? How do you think the experience was for the speaker? What was most challenging? What was easy?

Generalizing tip: Active listening can be done anytime. To further strengthen listening as well as memory skills, summarize the contents and context of the conversation briefly as part of your evening journaling exercise.

Counting Rice and Beans

✳ Relaxation Exercise   ⏱ *5 to 20 minutes*

A great way to force yourself to slow down at the end of the day is to enter into a mindless task that practices mindfulness while doing something repetitive, like counting. For this task, you'll need one cup of dried rice and another of dried beans or lentils, a piece of paper, and a pen or pencil. This exercise is helpful both as a mindful meditation and as a stress reducer; it also helps strengthen concentration skills.

STEPS:

1. At a table, mix the dried beans and rice into a pile. Make two columns on the paper—one for rice and one for beans.

2. Complete several mindful breath cycles with your eyes open or closed. Sit with your spine straight and your shoulders back. Do a short body scan. Breathe into any tension.

3. Start sorting the rice and beans into two piles by counting five grains of rice, then five beans. If you'd rather, sort one rice grain and one bean, or do five of each at a time. Once you've sorted out five, make five tally marks on your paper in each column.

4. Continue sorting and counting by fives until you sort the entire pile.

5. While you count and sort, remain mindful of only your breath and the task.

6. Once you finish, mix the piles back up. Here, you may choose to end the meditation. Or you can start it again, only this time count out 10 each time.

7. As you repeat this meditation, add an additional 10 to your count. Be sure to keep your spine straight and your shoulders back.

Let the Lantern Go

Many cultures release paper lanterns into the sky or onto the water as part of rituals and festivities. The practice carries many meanings—from good luck to family unity to releasing fears. This meditation can be a nice way to start or finish any other meditation. It can also help you drift off to sleep.

STEPS:

1. Close your eyes and inhale, bringing awareness to your breath. Hold the breath for two counts and, as you exhale, release any physical tension.

2. Repeat this mindful breath cycle 3 times.

3. On your fourth breath, call to mind something that's troubling you. Notice your thoughts, feelings, and physical sensations.

4. Now imagine standing on the bank of a gently flowing river at night. In your hands is a white paper lantern, lit from the inside. This lantern represents your ability to let go of your troubling thought or feeling. Don't attach judgment to this lantern. It just is.

5. Decide whether you will let it float on the river or float gently into the sky, then release the lantern.

6. As it floats away, it carries with it the thing that troubles you. Watch as the lantern gets smaller as it travels farther away, until you can no longer see it.

7. Once it's gone, inhale serenity into the space the trouble left behind. Exhale and open your eyes or keep them closed as you drift off to sleep.

Journaling the Mindful Month

✳ *Mindfulness Exercise*   ⊙ *10 minutes*

In the last chapter, you were introduced to a morning journaling practice that helped you set your intentions and let your mind run free. Evening journaling can help you reflect on the day's events and check in with your intentions for tomorrow. Or you can try a structured journaling exercise to strengthen mindfulness in particular areas.

I recommend focusing on a different area each month and spending 10 minutes in the evening answering the following questions in your journal, as they relate to that month's topic. I've listed some example topics here, but feel free to choose your own. I recommend evening journaling as part of a nightly sleep hygiene routine.

January: mindful exercise habits

February: mindful meditation practice

March: mindful listening

April: mindful relationships

May: mindfulness at work

June: mindful self-compassion

July: mindful spending

August: mindful caring for others

September: mindful impulse control

October: mindful eating

November: mindful gratitude

December: mindful gift giving

CONTINUED

STEPS:

1. Open your journal to the appropriate day.

2. Before you begin writing, draw in several deep breaths and focus on the topic that you'll be journaling about.

3. Reflect on your day and whether you had opportunities to practice mindfulness in this area. Answer the following questions in your journal:

   How was I able to be mindful in this area today?

   How did being mindful (or not) in this area impact my life today?

   How did that make me feel in the moment? How do I feel reflecting on it now?

   What prevented me from being mindful? Is there a way to change that?

   What, if anything, did I learn today as a result of being mindful in this area?

4. Feel free to create your own questions and freewrite anything that comes to mind. When you've finished, close your eyes and take several mindful breaths. Close your journal and continue with your sleep routine.

A Wonderful List

In my children's book, *My Whirling, Twirling Motor*, the parents help their child by writing down all the daily things he does "right" on a Wonderful List, which they read to him at bedtime. It's a way to reinforce for both the adult and the child that although ADHD causes noticeably difficult behavior that gets corrected all day, the child is also doing good things that just don't get noticed as often. This end-of-day exercise can remind you of the many wonderful things you probably don't give yourself credit for. Enjoy it as a standalone activity or add it to your evening journaling practice. You'll need a pen and paper, preferably a journal-style notebook.

STEPS:

1. Get into a comfortable position, close your eyes, and complete several mindful breath cycles.

2. Notice your emotions in this moment, whether negative or positive. Rate them on a scale of 1 to 100, with 100 being the most intense.

3. On an exhale, release any tight areas in your body and open your eyes.

4. With your pen and journal ready, jot down the emotions and their ratings from step 2, then go back over your day. Think of the different things you did during the day, from the mundane to the complex.

CONTINUED

5. Considering those moments, what did you do well? Did you say a kind word or hold the door open for someone? Did you complete a task in less time than you had before? Did you check off an item on your to-do list? Did you practice mindfulness?

6. List what you did well in your journal, no matter how inconsequential. As you write, remember to breathe with awareness.

7. Keep going until you can't think of anything more to add to your list.

8. Read the list aloud starting with, *Today, I* . . .

9. When you've finished reading, check back in on the intensity of the emotions you rated before you started. Jot down the numbers now, trying not to judge whether they increased or decreased.

10. Continue with your journaling. When you've finished, take several closing breaths and release any physical or emotional tension you may be carrying so you can sleep well.

Tomorrow and Tomorrow

⁂ *Executive Functioning Exercise*   ⏲ *10 minutes*

When it comes to executive functioning challenges, the Boy Scouts have the right idea: be prepared. Preparation blends mindfulness with concentration, organization, and intention, and ensures that we have at least a shot at accomplishing our goals without the stress of winging it. For productive tomorrows, add this 10-minute preparation exercise to the end of your days. You'll need either a paper or digital calendar/planner and to-do list. If these are not tools you already use, consider adding them to help with managing many ADHD symptoms. This exercise should not be part of your sleep routine, so do it outside of the hour before bed.

STEPS:

1. Sit with your spine straight, close your eyes, and draw in several mindful breaths. As you exhale, breathe out any residual stress you might be carrying from your day. Envision it floating out of you, riding the wave of your breath.

2. Open your eyes and open your calendar and to-do list.

3. Look at the events scheduled for tomorrow. Note their times.

4. For each event, close your eyes and imagine yourself doing whatever is scheduled. Set an intention for the event. Here are some examples:

   I will arrive on time.

   I will bring my A-game to this meeting.

   I will have a positive attitude.

CONTINUED

5. Look at your to-do list. Mark the items you hope to finish tomorrow. Imagine yourself doing those items.

6. While you imagine the events, if tension enters your body or worries enter your mind, it's okay. Notice them and breathe into the feelings.

7. During this exercise, if you realize you need to notify someone of a schedule change, write a quick reminder note, and finish the exercise.

8. When you've finished going through your items, close your eyes and complete three mindful breath cycles.

Winding Down

Sleep can be a challenging beast. A study from the Netherlands indicates that the production of melatonin at nightfall is delayed for people with ADHD. Late melatonin production results in a circadian rhythm, or internal clock, in which both the start and end of the natural sleep cycle are delayed. The following ritual can help establish healthy sleep hygiene and remove some common blocks to melatonin production, leading to a more regulated circadian rhythm. Following the same sleep routine each night sends a signal to your brain that it's time to wind down. If you don't have time for all of this every night, it's okay. A shorter ritual will help, too. Sweet dreams!

STEPS:

1. Light is one of the greatest contributors and inhibitors to melatonin production, as the body takes its cues from the presence of the sun. Although this is an evening meditation, we lay its foundation in the morning. Do your morning meditation while soaking in the sun's rays—this helps produce serotonin, which helps produce melatonin earlier in the evening.

2. After nightfall, watch your light intake. Cue your body by dimming the lights, and stay off your phone and computer for at least an hour before bedtime. The blue light from your screen sends a signal to your brain not to produce melatonin. (If you must look at a screen, try amber-tinted glasses, which can be found online and block blue light.)

CONTINUED

3. Drink something warm. Numerous teas claim to promote sleep. Although I can't speak to their efficacy, if you enjoy any warm, noncaffeinated beverage within an hour before you go to sleep, your brain will eventually associate it with bedtime.

4. In the hour before bed, remain mindful of your breath and check in with your thoughts. Use some of the techniques from chapter 6, Calm the Emotions, to reframe stressful thoughts as more positive ones.

5. Take a warm bath. Increasing body heat causes your body to work harder to keep you cool. Your heart and metabolic rates increase, which naturally tires you. Additionally, a bath is a great place to practice mindful breathing, which may reduce stress and overstimulating thoughts.

6. Use aromatherapy, specifically lavender. A study done at Kagoshima University shows that linalool, a substance present in lavender, has a calming effect when inhaled. Lavender essential oils can be added to a bath or used in a diffuser. Some facial creams are scented with lavender.

7. Reconsider watching TV before bed as the light from the screen can keep you awake. Instead, read something not too emotionally activating and/or do an end-of-day meditation. The Body Scan 101 meditation (page 44) can be particularly helpful to relax the body and mind.

8. When you're ready to shut your eyes, set your intention by telling your pillow that it's time to sleep.

Generalizing tip: *During the day, check your caffeine intake. Too much caffeine can inhibit sleep later. Some foods, such as eggs, milk, fish, and nuts, are higher in melatonin, and a few studies indicate that eating these foods may contribute to melatonin production. If you have children (with or without ADHD) with sleep issues, consider introducing a similar nighttime routine.*

CHAPTER NINE

5-MINUTE

Sometimes five minutes is all we have for our mindfulness practice. For someone with ADHD, sometimes five minutes is all we can tolerate! The following meditations are short and sweet and designed to provide as much mindfulness bang for your buck as longer, sitting meditations.

Five Postures

✿ *Mindfulness Exercise*　　　　　　　　🕐 *5 minutes*

When time and restlessness are an issue, use these quick steps to ground yourself using five important aspects of your meditation posture. This exercise should be done in a comfortable seated position with your spine drawn upright.

STEPS:

1. **Gaze:** Soften your eyelids and let your gaze drop softly. Spend 1 minute aware of your gaze while breathing mindfully.

2. **Shoulders:** Keep your spine upright, being careful not to hunch, slouch, or raise your shoulders. Breathe mindfully into your shoulders for 1 minute.

3. **Chin:** Tuck your chin slightly, moving it down an inch. Keep your head and neck straight but relaxed. Breathe into your chin for 1 minute.

4. **Jaw:** Open and close your mouth, stretching your jaw muscles. Move your jaw slowly side to side, being careful not to overextend it. Relax the jaw muscles, breathing into them for 1 minute.

5. **Hands:** Shake your hands vigorously. Let them rest on your lap or by your sides. Breathe into your hands for 1 minute.

Give-and-Take

It's easy to get lost in our own problems and suffering. One of the best ways to ease that suffering is by helping others who are less fortunate. Giving to others creates endorphins in the brain that can promote an instant feel-good sensation. It also puts our problems in perspective and creates a sense of belonging by connecting us to other people. These quick steps can shift our focus away from our own suffering and offer a jolt of compassion and calm.

STEPS:

1. Begin 2 minutes of mindful breathing.

2. Prepare by inhaling visual sensations such as darkness, heat, or weight. It may be helpful to imagine yourself thirsty in the desert or stuck in a dark elevator. Breathe the discomfort to your core.

3. When you exhale, imagine releasing the opposite, such as bright light, coolness, or levity. Imagine being doused in water in the desert or flooded with bright light pouring in through open elevator doors.

4. Next, focus on someone's pain. The pain can be overt, such as an illness or deep depression, or it can be the quiet suffering of some-one who feels inadequate. As you inhale, draw in that suffering. Visualize the relief felt by the other with this suffering removed.

5. As you exhale, give them the opposite of their pain, visualizing their body and mind filling with love.

Generalizing tip: *Switch the meditation up by focusing on someone who has upset you in the past. You may be surprised at what shifts in you when you do.*

Smiling Is a Two-Way Street

✽ *Compassion Exercise* ⏲ *5 minutes*

This meditation is good when you're feeling low or upset with yourself. Just as our emotional state influences our facial muscles into forming a smile or frown, so, too, can our facial muscles influence our emotional state.

STEPS:

1. Stand in front of a mirror.

2. Smile softly, as if you're meeting yourself and want to make a nice impression.

3. Complete 4 mindful breath cycles, keeping the soft smile.

4. Look at yourself without judgment. Say encouraging words while continuing to smile.

5. Smile widely as if you heard something funny.

6. Let out a forced laugh. Continue laughing for at least 10 seconds.

7. Do an internal check and notice how you feel. At first, you might feel inauthentic. But as you continue to smile, you may find that your mood begins to shift.

Generalizing tip: The next time you're in a bad mood, smile. It may soften your feelings and positively impact the feelings of those around you.

Fight the Power

✻ Cognitive Exercise   ⓘ *5 minutes*

We often assign power and truth to negative thoughts, due to the brain's threat defense system. Positive thoughts don't get a similar respect, as we frequently discount their veracity and weight. In cognitive therapy, there's a trick to defusing the bomb of negative thoughts—it's called "cognitive defusion." In this exercise, we'll focus on negative self-talk and take away its power by reframing the language we use to describe it.

STEPS:

1. Begin with a minute of mindful breathing, focusing on your breath and body.

2. Next, invite any common negative remarks you use to judge yourself.

   I'm so stupid.

   I never do anything right.

   I'm always spacing out.

   I'm so messy.

3. Notice the tension that settles into your body as these thoughts are invited in. Breathe into it and release it.

CONTINUED

4. Rephrase the thoughts as just thoughts.

   I'm having the thought that I'm stupid.

   I'm having the thought that I never do anything right.

   I'm having the thought that I always space out.

   I'm having the thought that I'm so messy.

5. Framing negative self-talk as simply a thought helps put space between it and you. Instead of a truth, it's only a thought.

6. Notice any tension in your body as you rephrase these thoughts. Is it greater or less than it was before? Breathe into it. Let the tension and the thoughts go.

Generalizing tip: *Try being mindful in the moment when you use this self-talk during your daily life. Catch it and rephrase it. It takes practice, but doing so can help shift the way you view yourself.*

Swinging from Tree to Tree

✤ Mindfulness Exercise   ⏱ *5 minutes*

Change can be difficult for people who struggle with executive functioning. That's because the area of the brain that moves us from task to task isn't receiving enough neurotransmitter fuel to easily shift gears. If you're hyper-focusing and unable to transition, this visualization exercise can boost your ability to flexibly focus. It's typically done at a time and place where you hyper-focus frequently.

STEPS:

1. Post a small sign in your hyper-focus area as a reminder to do this visualization. You can write "Tree Swinging," or, if you're feeling creative, draw a monkey as a cue.

2. When your eye catches your cue, check in with yourself. Are you hyper-focused in this moment?

3. If the answer is yes, note how this hyper-focused state feels in your body.

4. Breathe. Visualize a monkey getting ready to swing from one tree to the next on a vine. This monkey represents your focus.

5. As you exhale, picture the monkey swinging easily to the next tree. This represents your focus shifting from the task you're on now to the next one.

6. Every time you notice your cue, do this momentary visualization and body check.

7. When the next transition comes, breathe, visualize the monkey swinging, and when it lands on the next tree, picture it releasing the vine and, with it, you of your task.

Serenity Prayer with a Twist

⚘ Mantra Exercise   ⏱ *5 minutes*

We know that repeating a mantra can shift neural pathways. One of the most well-known verses used this way is the Serenity Prayer, written by theologian Reinhold Niebuhr in the 1930s and frequently cited in 12-step programs. It reminds us where to place our focus—on that which we can change. You may use the verse as written or substitute words as in the following example.

SERENITY PRAYER:

God, grant me the serenity

to accept the things I cannot change,

the courage to change the things I can,

and the wisdom to know the difference.

YOUR POSSIBLE VERSION:

Grant me the serenity

to accept that I cannot change my physiology,

the courage to change my strategies,

and the wisdom to forgive myself.

Use your verse as part of a quick mantra meditation or repeat it throughout your day. Repeat the mantra for five minutes, without being distracted, taking in a mindful breath in between repetitions.

Triple Piko Breath

This meditation is inspired by Hawaiian culture, where the word *piko* represents three centers of the body—the crown of the head, the navel, and the reproductive areas, which connect us to the past, present, and future, respectively. The head connects us to beliefs and values of people that came before us. The navel is a connection to our immediate family. The reproductive organs connect us to future offspring. Breathing into these areas can be a quick way to ground yourself in connection, or *ohana*, in a moment when you may feel lonely and/or need some spiritual, emotional, or physical grounding. In Hawaiian, *ohana* means "family" and extends to the greater sense of anyone who is meaningful in your life.

STEPS:

1. Relax your body and breathe into the crown of your head. As you do, visualize a supportive person from your past, and breathe in their love and support.

2. As you exhale, breathe out gratitude for their presence in your life.

3. Next, breathe into your navel. Picture the people in your life you're connected to, and breathe in their love and support. As you exhale, breathe out gratitude for their presence in your life.

4. Now breathe into your reproductive area. Breathe in a connection to those who will come after you. As you exhale, breathe out the ways that you may offer them love and support.

5. Repeat this cycle as often as you find helpful until you are ready to move on.

Breath Matching

✿ *Mindfulness Exercise*   ◷ *5 minutes*

Most of our mindfulness exercises anchor themselves in our breath. But we're not alone in our breath—those around us breathe, too, and we can use their breath to deepen our mindfulness as well. This practice uses another human or animal to bring awareness to your breath through theirs. It's ideally done with a close companion, but anyone's breath will work.

STEPS:

1. Ground yourself in the steps of a basic meditation.

2. Sit or stand close enough to another human or animal to see the rise and fall of their chest as they breathe.

3. If it's a close companion, sit near enough to hear their breath.

4. Can you match the rhythm of their breathing? Is it faster or slower than yours?

5. How long are you able to keep pace with them before it feels uncomfortable? Notice where you feel any discomfort. In your chest, abdomen, or nostrils?

6. If you can, lean in and place your ear on their chest. Can you hear the air as it rushes in and out of their lungs?

7. Continue matching their breath rhythm, bringing your focus back to their breath and yours whenever you sense your mind wandering.

Generalizing tip: *This exercise can be done using the breath of anyone nearby, or you can find breath sounds online, including here: YouTube.com/watch?v=1x0zn7lwpbY.*

Dantian Meditation

Similar to the Hawaiian *piko* centers and Indian yogic chakras, *dantian* are Taoist energy centers thought to be located in three areas of the body:

Shen: the head, representing your spirit and intelligence

Qi: the chest, representing your spark of life

Jing: the lower abdomen, representing your essence

The following is a breath meditation that may rejuvenate your *chi*—your energy current—when any of your centers are running on empty.

STEPS:

1. Use basic meditation to ground yourself in your body and breath.

2. Bring your awareness to the center of your forehead. Imagine a glowing, *dantian* ball to represent your spirit and intelligence.

3. Inhale into this ball until it's so large it envelops you. As you inhale, imagine the ball inflating and its glow intensifying. As you exhale, visualize its glow waning, but only slightly.

4. Move to the *dantian* ball in your chest. This ball represents your life force. Repeat steps 2 and 3.

5. Move to the *dantian* ball in your lower abdomen. This ball represents your essence. Repeat steps 2 and 3.

6. Once all three centers envelop your body, bring your awareness to your overall energy. With your next exhalation, send the light from your *dantian* out into the world.

Even Monstrous Thoughts Need a Hug

⁂ Mindfulness Exercise   ⏱ *5 minutes*

Sometimes we have negative and judgmental thoughts toward ourselves and others. These thoughts generally stem from a place of pain. They are your monster. A mindfulness practice helps us notice these "monstrous" thoughts, but then what do we do with them? As you strengthen your awareness skills, use this exercise to help move past self-judgment toward self-compassion.

STEPS:

1. In a moment when you've noticed unhelpful, negative, or judgmental thoughts, stop what you're doing and close your eyes.

2. Take in a deep, mindful breath.

3. Instead of chiding yourself for the thought, understand that it represents pain. Picture the thought as a monster who has hurt itself. Imagine hugging it, as you might console someone in pain. Wrap your arms around this monster, actively telling it, "You need a hug."

4. Squeeze it tightly.

5. When you're ready, release the hug.

6. As you release the hug, release the "monstrous" thought and carry on.

What's in Your Sensory Box?

⁂ Stress Reduction Exercise   ⏱ *5 to 20 minutes*

When I work with children who struggle with big emotional reactions, one suggestion for their parents is to create a sensory box that incorporates something for each of the five senses. When we're feeling emotionally dysregulated, accessing our five senses can be another way, in addition to breath, to calm the body and mind. To prepare for this exercise, you'll fill a small container with items that appeal to your five senses—something pleasing to look at, something that smells nice, something that feels good to touch, something that tastes good, and something that sounds soothing. Keep this container in a readily available place.

STEPS:

1. When you're feeling upset, take a quiet moment with your container.

2. Close your eyes and take several mindful breaths.

3. When you're ready, open the container.

4. Spend a minute with each item, as if it's the first time you've ever experienced it.

5. Note how each sense reacts to this item. Breathe into the sensation.

6. When you're ready, close the container. Breathe one full cycle and put the container away.

Sensing as You Go

⁂ Stress Reduction Exercise　　　　　　　⏱ *5 minutes*

In the last meditation, we used items that stimulated individual senses to help regulate stress. But we may not always have access to those items. The good news is that wherever you go, your five senses go with you, and you can use them to ground you in moments of dysregulation.

STEPS:

1. When you're upset or stressed, breathe into your navel for a count of four, hold the breath for a count of four, then exhale for a count of four.

2. As you continue your rhythmic breaths, notice sounds for the next minute. Reach beyond the sounds immediately around you to ones farther away.

3. For the next minute, notice what you are touching. Are you doing anything with your hands? How does your clothing feel? Your shoes? Your hair?

4. Now notice odors. Breathing in through your nose for a minute, can you smell anything?

5. What do you see? Extend your gaze for the next minute, truly noticing the details, colors, and sizes of things that you can see.

6. Taste is next. You may not be eating, so notice if your mouth is dry. Swallow, and lick your teeth with your tongue. Spend the next minute exploring the inside of your mouth, breathing through it, noticing how the air feels as it passes through.

7. Take a closing mindful breath and consider how you feel now.

Five Things around You

✲ Mindfulness Exercise   *⊙ 5 minutes*

This meditation is similar to the previous one, but this one focuses solely on vision as your grounding tool.

STEPS:

1. Remembering your breath, take the next 5 minutes to notice 5 things around you. Anything.

2. Pick your first thing. Tell yourself what it is.

   That is a pen.

3. Take it in as if it's the first time you've ever seen anything like it. Describe it to yourself, noticing its color variations, shape, and details.

   This pen is black.

   It's six inches long, and its cap connects almost at its center.

   There's white writing on the side.

   It has a metal clip.

4. Breathe. Feel a sense of awe at the object and its use.

5. After a minute, move to your next object and repeat steps 3 and 4.

6. Repeat as needed for all objects. As you finish, notice if your feelings have changed since you began this meditation. Breathe into them. Release your breath and continue your day.

Learning to Help Yourself Out of Your Cage

✿ *Mindfulness Exercise* ⏱ *5 minutes*

In the 1960s, an (awful) study was done on caged dogs that showed how animals learn to feel helpless when they repeatedly try something that doesn't work. One thing they learned, however, was that this learned helplessness can be unlearned. Often children with ADHD grow up with a similar sense of learned helplessness—either from well-meaning adults who do everything for them or from frequent attempts and failures. This meditation is a moment to focus on areas of your life where you've always assumed you "can't" and to challenge that sense of helplessness.

STEPS:

1. Use basic meditation to ground yourself.

2. Bring your awareness to something you know you cannot do. This is your cage. This cage prevents you from doing the thing you know you cannot do.

3. Visualize this cage. Answer the following questions:

   - Who put you in this cage? How long have you been inside?

   - Who set the rules of this cage, determining that you "cannot"?

   - Is this cage to protect you from others, others from you, or you from yourself?

   - Is it locked? Who holds the key?

   - What would happen if the cage door were to open? What's preventing you from opening it?

Fake It 'til You Make It

⚕ Emotional Regulation Exercise   ⏱ *5 minutes*

There's an expression in neuroscience that states, "Neurons that fire together, wire together." The phrase was coined by Dr. Donald Hebb, a neuropsychologist who pioneered our understanding of human behavior and the brain. He determined that the repeated firing of one neuron—say, being frequently bored at work—alongside the firing of another—that boredom is an uncomfortable feeling—creates a strong connection: work is always a bad place. "Uncoupling" these neurons can be difficult. One way to do so, though, is to force the firing of a new neuron by "faking it" until the associated neuron "makes it" to a more positive, helpful thought. The following is an active meditation to rewire your misbehaving neurons.

STEPS:

1. When you're facing a difficult task or experience, take a moment to close your eyes and complete a mindful breath cycle.

2. What are you feeling in this moment, physically and emotionally?

3. Imagine how you'd like to feel instead.

4. If you're bored, imagine yourself excited. If you're sad, imagine yourself happy. If you're angry, imagine yourself accepting.

5. Breathe into this new feeling. Would you move your body differently with this new feeling? If you're slouched, would you stand tall? If your arms are crossed, would you open them?

CONTINUED

6. On an inhalation, embody the opposite of your true feeling. If this is difficult, imagine you're a child playacting. You're purposefully faking your feelings in this moment, even though it might be hard.

7. Attempt to maintain this fake feeling through your task or experience.

8. Anchor your breath as a reminder to stay in this fake feeling. If you wander and lapse into your true feeling, shift back without judgment.

9. You may only be able to last a couple of minutes or even seconds in this fake feeling, but with practice, you'll begin to feel the new neurons wiring together.

10. Take a closing breath and notice if your body and mind feel any different.

CHAPTER TEN

MOVEMENT

In previous chapters, we established the important connection between the mind and the body as an active two-way street. If you're struggling with the mindfulness practices that require your body to be still, feel free to literally shake things up with the practices from this chapter, all of which incorporate movement and mindfulness.

Mindful Workout

☀ Mindfulness Exercise   ⏱ *5 minutes*

Whether you exercise regularly or every once in a while, chances are good that you zone out when working out. The thing is, practicing mindfulness when exercising can increase the intensity and effectiveness of your workout.

STEPS:

1. Before beginning your workout, take a moment to close your eyes and breathe. While breathing mindfully, visualize your workout. Picture yourself working to your maximum potential and enjoying it.

2. Open your eyes and begin your workout. While exercising, mindfully take regular deep breaths to oxygenate your cells.

3. Notice your muscles—particularly the ones you're stressing. Breathe into those areas. Notice the secondary muscles as they support the rest of your body. Are you carrying tension anywhere? If you could be working harder but aren't, don't judge yourself. Take it at your own pace.

4. As you near the end of your routine, check whether you have the energy to push harder or if you might hurt yourself if you do. Be mindful of that choice.

5. Upon finishing, complete several closing breath cycles. Notice that it's difficult to regulate your breath due to your increased need for oxygen.

6. Check in with your physical and emotional sensations. Note whether you feel better, worse, or any different than before you began. Try not to attach any judgment to those feelings.

Shake, Shake, Shake

✴ *Calming Exercise*   ⏱ *5 minutes*

If you're too restless to meditate, you might want to try some vigorous shaking. For this meditation, you'll want to wear comfortable clothes and shoes (barefoot is okay, too). You'll also need a bit of room and privacy (if you care about that).

STEPS:

1. While standing, draw in a deep breath and blow it out with force through your nose or mouth.

2. Begin jumping up and down. If it helps, imagine there is a jump rope keeping you in motion.

3. After ensuring you can stretch your arms without hitting anything, begin to wave. Let your arms flop as if there were no bones inside them.

4. Let your tongue wag, keeping your mouth open. Remember to continue breathing.

5. Move your upper body around while you continue to jump and flop your arms.

6. Move your head if your neck is strong enough.

7. Blow raspberries, make popping noises, even consider yelling. Get your energy out in whatever way moves you.

8. After 5 minutes, take a big, cleansing breath. Check your feelings and your physical sensations. Now you're ready to move into your meditation.

Generalizing tip: *This exercise can sometimes help if you wake up in the middle of the night and have trouble falling back asleep.*

Kiss the Earth with Your Feet

✳ Mindfulness Exercise   ⏲ *10 minutes*

Vietnamese Buddhist monk Thich Nhat Hanh is quoted as having said, "When we walk like [we are rushing], we print anxiety and sorrow on the Earth. We have to walk in a way that we only print peace and serenity on the Earth. . . . Be aware of the contact between your feet and the Earth. Walk as if you are kissing the Earth with your feet." Zen walking, whether it's across the kitchen, from the car to the store, or on a purposeful hike, can connect the mind and body with their surroundings. We might not always have the time to slow down and kiss the earth, but the exercise that follows can help you generalize the practice as you walk through your day. For this meditation, you'll need space. I encourage practicing outside. Barefoot is best, but please be mindful of safety.

STEPS:

1. With enough space to take at least 10 unobstructed steps, stand with your feet firmly planted, hip-width apart. Relax your shoulders and let your arms fall heavy at your sides. Center your head over your straight spine.

2. With your eyes soft, take 3 mindful breaths.

3. Place your hands in a position called *shashu mudra*—a fist at your chest, cupped by your other hand. Walk slowly and softly in a straight line, heel to toe, for anywhere from 10 to 40 paces.

4. Breathe with each soft step, focusing on your breath and the feeling of your feet on the earth. Is the ground soft or hard? Warm or cool?

5. Focus on your lower extremities, bringing awareness to the seamless connection between your brain's will and your legs' movement. As you walk, label your movements.

   My heel is landing on the ground; now my toes are.

   My left leg is drawing forward.

6. Center your core as though you're on an imaginary tightrope. Is it difficult to balance?

7. Notice if your mind wanders from your feet and gently return it. Consider using this time to repeat a helpful mantra.

8. When you reach the end of your straight line, turn and walk back.

9. Imagine now that with each step, you're connecting with the ground as if you are "kissing" it with your feet. This earth holds you on your journey through life. Express gratitude for it.

10. Continue walking back and forth, slowly and mindfully, while passing peace and serenity back and forth between you and the ground until you're ready to end this exercise.

Forest Bathing

⚘ Stress Reduction Exercise   *🕐 20 minutes*

In the 1980s, a form of eco-therapy emerged in Japan called *shinrin-yoku*, which literally means "forest wellness." Since then, this practice of stress reduction via a walk in the woods has been coined "forest bathing" in the West. Studies conducted all over the world show that being in, and even simply looking at, nature creates numerous health benefits. As little as 15 minutes can have a positive effect on the nervous system, reducing stress and increasing attention, creativity, and social connection. This meditation is ideally done in a forest. If you're unsure where to go, try searching the internet for trails in your area.

STEPS:

1. Consider going to the forest outside of peak times to ensure it's quiet.

2. Remember to silence your phone and consider leaving pets at home.

3. If you're with a companion, agree not to engage in conversation during your meditation.

4. As you begin, remember to breathe mindfully. Your focus during this time should be on mindful breathing and the sensations of the forest around you.

5. Notice if your thoughts wander to your to-do list, your concerns, or your goals. Return to your breath.

6. Your presence in this forest will change the environment. Notice if the behavior of any animals and insects changes as you move.

7. At a certain point, stand still. Locate something you can see that makes no sound. Hone in on its details, letting your eyes wander over it slowly.

8. Next, locate something you can hear but not see. Isolate the sound from others and listen to it intently. Then expand your awareness. How many different sounds do you hear? Can you recognize the absence of machine-made sounds? Do you feel different as a result?

9. Continue walking, inhaling the aromas around you. Can you recognize any smells?

10. The surrounding trees take in your carbon dioxide and create the oxygen you breathe. You're part of nature's give-and-take. Accept the gift of air from the forest with gratitude as you inhale, and as you exhale, offer it your gift of breath.

11. Keeping the spirit of the previous walking meditation in mind, place your feet on the ground gently and mindfully, "kissing the earth" with your feet as you move.

12. If you walked with a friend, when you finish, share one moment or memory from your experience.

Generalizing tip: If it's not possible to access nature, try searching the internet using the term "forest bathing" for videos of forests and sounds. Play these sounds in the background while you work on a stressful project to keep you relaxed and attuned to your task. You might also consider looking at nature photos. Studies show that even just looking at nature photographs has a positive impact on cognition and mood.

Dancing, *Katsugen Undo* Style

   Stress Reduction Exercise   ⏱ *15 minutes*

Katsugen undo is a type of movement developed by Japanese healer Haruchika Noguchi, as a way of releasing energy that he believed inhibited a balance of the autonomic nervous system. Instead of doing purposeful, controlled movement, *katsugen undo* gives the body free rein to move impulsively. If you're frequently trying to curb impulsive movement, an exercise that allows the body to do what it wants can feel liberating. This exercise is based on Noguchi's practice, but it incorporates music to facilitate the experience. Try it with or without music but with plenty of space to move. This can be practiced alone or with friends and family—especially young children.

STEPS:

1. Clear an area, and if you're using music, turn it on.

2. Standing with your eyes closed, place your hands on your abdomen and draw in a breath, feeling your belly move with the inhalation.

3. As you exhale, forcefully drop your hands and make the sound "Ha!"

4. With arms at your sides, relax your shoulders and keep your spine straight.

5. Listen to the music. Feel the sensations in your body. Are you able to feel the rhythm of the music or the resonance of the bass?

6. Let your body respond. Try not to control it (unless you're in a limited area), allowing your body to move to the music.

7. Don't hold back. Let your energy flow into your extremities and into your vocal cords, and move and sing or vocalize as your body chooses.

8. Initially, you may feel silly and reserved. Don't judge yourself.

9. Continue for as long as the energy flows. Your movements may be small and repetitive or large and wild. They may eventually slow and stop.

10. When your body chooses to end the exercise, bring your hands to your abdomen, and after an inhale, breathe out a soft humming sound.

Don't Move!

✲ *Mindfulness Exercise*　　　　　　　 ⏱ *5 minutes*

In the last exercise, we allowed our impulsive bodies to move wildly and without judgment. In real life, we don't always have that liberty. People with ADHD frequently struggle to stay seated for dinner, a TV show, or a family game night and constantly get up to do something. This exercise challenges us to bring awareness to our movement and discomfort and to exert control over our bodies when an excess buildup of energy has seemingly hijacked our muscles. It's best done during your regular day, outside of time reserved for meditation.

STEPS:

1. When your body is particularly antsy and wants to move, notice the feeling. What movement does it want to make?

2. Why do you feel the urge to move? Is it to pass the time or to get more comfortable? Or do you just *have* to move?

3. Notice the sensation but resist the urge. Relax and breathe into it, remaining still.

4. Once you've noticed the urge, it's no longer a mindless one and is now part of your present-moment experience.

5. What does it feel like not to move? Are you uncomfortable? Can you sit with this discomfort and acknowledge it?

6. Do you feel in control of your body, or is it the other way around?

7. Repeat to yourself: *I'm in control of my body. I may be uncomfortable, but it will pass. I don't have to move.*

8. Continue to breathe into the feeling until it passes.

Tug of War with a Monster

⁂ *Stress Reduction Exercise*   ⏱ *5 minutes*

The following exercise is based on an intervention in acceptance and commitment therapy, which highlights a different option to the incessant struggle against our monstrous thoughts and feelings. For this meditation, you'll need something strong like a rope and something sturdy to tie it to, like a doorknob or fence post.

STEPS:

1. Tie your rope to something strong.

2. Gripping the rope tightly, step back so it's taut, keeping one leg in front of the other, like in tug-of-war stance.

3. Close your eyes, take 3 mindful breaths, then pull.

4. Imagine you're pulling against a vicious monster trying to drag you into a hole. This monster represents struggle and pain and any negative thoughts that terrorize you. What does this monster look and smell like? What sound does it make?

5. Pull hard, fighting against the feeling this monster causes. What does it feel like to pull? Is it tiring? Does it feel futile? Do you feel powerless?

6. This monster will continue to terrorize you the more you engage with it. How successful can you be in this fight?

7. Continue to pull, and repeat to yourself: *I don't have to fight this monster. I have a choice.*

8. Abruptly drop the rope.

9. Draw in a deep breath.

CONTINUED

10. How does your body feel having dropped the rope? How does your mind feel? Do you feel tense or relaxed, powerful or drained?

11. Notice that by simply dropping the rope, the negative thoughts, struggles, and pain don't magically disappear. But the exhausting fight does.

12. Close your eyes and take three mindful breaths. As you breathe, open your mind to other options for fighting this monster.

The Balance of Power

.⁎. *Movement Exercise*   ⏱ *10 minutes*

Proprioception is the awareness of the body's position and movement through space, and it's often a struggle for people with ADHD. We feel a general sense of clumsiness, and not without reason. Scans show that ADHD often comes with differences in the areas of the brain responsible for movement, coordination, and spatial awareness. I've walked into countless doorframes, and I've had child clients suddenly fall over from a standing position, simply because they momentarily lost balance! This meditation can help increase mindfulness of your proprioception, which can help you exert power over it. You'll need a chair or wall or something hip height to hold on to.

STEPS:

1. Stand next to your support object with your legs hip-width apart.

2. Close your eyes, letting your arms hang loosely at your sides. Drop your shoulders and feel the heaviness in your feet as gravity keeps them anchored.

3. Draw three mindful breaths into your abdomen, bringing awareness to your core.

4. Your core plays a vital role in balance. Tighten it and hold for one breath. Notice if you feel more or less centered with a tight core.

5. With your eyes still closed and your core and arms relaxed, simply stand. Notice if your body has a natural tendency to lean in a certain direction. See if you can center your body and keep it there with little exertion.

CONTINUED

6. Open your eyes and repeat step 5. Is it different with your eyes open?

7. With your eyes closed, purposefully lean in the direction your body wants to. How far can you lean without having to step in that direction to regain your balance? Remember, this is a practice of noticing, not necessarily strengthening.

8. Repeat step 7 with your eyes open and notice if it feels different, then breathe.

9. Grip your support object with the hand that's closest to it. Breathe into the grip. Notice if you feel more grounded with this support.

10. Imagine the foot next to the support object has sprouted roots, is anchored deeply into the ground, and that the outside foot is tied to a cloud. Close your eyes. As you inhale, raise the outside foot, either in front or to the side, supporting yourself with only the anchored foot and your grip on the object.

11. Hold for one breath and, if you can, let go of the support for your next breath.

12. Repeat steps 10 and 11 with your eyes open, keeping your awareness on how your body balances itself, then turn and do the other side, remembering to breathe through each movement.

13. Each time you practice this meditation, add a breath cycle to each movement, extending the practice and strengthening your power to balance.

Forward Folding

Yogis believe that folding the body forward so the torso hangs upside down has many health benefits for the body and mind. It can relieve stress and fatigue, increase blood flow, stretch the hips and legs, and stimulate the liver, kidneys, and digestive system. Personally, after I hang in a forward bend, I feel invigorated with an improved appreciation for the right-side-up world around me. This meditation can be useful if you need a quick pick-me-up during a boring task. It's also just a nice way to start the day.

STEPS:

1. Stand with your legs hip-width apart and your hands in a prayer position at your chest. You'll need enough space around you to stretch your arms.

2. Take a breath into your core, and as you exhale, raise your hands, palms facing front, over your head.

3. As you inhale again, bring your arms down to your sides and, at the same time, slowly fold your torso forward. Be mindful of your back and hamstrings (the muscle in the back of your thighs), and bend forward as far as you comfortably can without strain.

4. Bring your hands to meet your feet, bending your knees if need be. Let your head drop and relax your neck.

5. In this folded position, breathe into your middle; comfortably straighten your legs if you can.

6. Feel free to let your arms dangle loosely or wrap them around the back of your knees.

CONTINUED

7. Breathe into this position, bringing awareness to any discomfort. Make any physical adjustments.

8. When you're ready to stand up, inhale and starting at the base of your spine, begin to raise your torso one vertebrae at a time.

9. Be careful not to rise too quickly. The blood may not reach your brain as fast, and you could faint.

10. Raise your arms so that as you reach an upright position, they're extended straight overhead.

11. Inhale again and, as you exhale, bring your hands back to the prayer position.

12. Notice how your body and mind feel after spending time upside down. Center yourself with a closing breath.

Cat, Cow, Child

✻ *Movement Exercise*   ⏱ *10 minutes*

The superhighway that is your spinal cord is bathed in a liquid called cerebrospinal fluid, or CSF. CSF circulates through the central nervous system, bringing crucial nutrients to the brain and removing waste, important for the brain's overall functioning, and also acting as an important protective cushion. The following yoga meditation helps activate the spine in time with the breath, promoting healthy movement of CFS—plus, it feels good! You may need a mat, towel, or carpet to comfortably do this exercise.

STEPS:

1. Get down on all fours. With your head and spine in a neutral position, draw a mindful breath into your navel and exhale.

2. On your next inhale, arch your back as if you're a scared cat. Arch only to your spine's comfort level.

3. As you exhale, lower your spine to a concave shape, like that of an old farm cow.

4. Notice how this gentle stretch of the spine feels. Do you feel a strain anywhere, such as in your wrists, neck, or knees? Make any necessary adjustments.

5. Continue this pattern, getting into the cat pose as you inhale and the cow pose as you exhale, for at least 10 breath cycles.

6. When you finish, drop your bottom onto your feet and touch your forehead to the floor. Extend your arms beyond your head, letting them rest on the ground.

7. This is called child's pose and should be a restful position. Remain here for as long as you like.

CHAPTER ELEVEN

DO ANYWHERE

The miscellaneous meditations and exercises in this chapter are mostly quick and can be done on the fly, although some do require supplies and are not typical meditations. As you progress in the sitting meditations from the previous chapters, you may wish to incorporate some of these less traditional variations into your practice.

Hands on the Wheel

꙼ *Mindful Exercise*   ⏱ *5 to 20 minutes*

When we drive frequently and to the same places, it's easy, especially with ADHD, to lapse into autopilot as our minds wander and our bodies take over the task of driving. This can be dangerous. Use this meditation when you're the driver, or the passenger, to train your brain to be mindful in the car.

STEPS:

1. Before you enter the car, with your hand on the door handle, remind yourself of your destination.

2. Once you're in the car, before you turn it on, check your body and set your intentions.

3. Once you're on the road, feel your hands on the steering wheel and take a deep breath. If you're a passenger, place one hand on the interior of the car, such as the door or seat. Do you feel the vibration of the motor? Notice your grip and where your hands are placed. How do they feel?

4. Taking care not to get too lost in the hum of the motor, remind yourself again of your destination.

5. Safely notice the vehicles around you. Without taking your eyes off the road, notice the color of the cars. What color do you see most?

6. Remind yourself again of your destination.

7. Check in with your other senses. How does the car smell? Are you playing music? Is the motor loud? Be careful not to get too lost in your other senses.

8. Throughout this mindfulness practice, remind yourself of your destination and remember your breath. Safe travels.

The Empty Chair

Gestalt therapy, established by Fritz Perls in the 1940s, practices an exercise known as "empty chair" to help people achieve a different perspective on both internal and external conflicts. People with ADHD can sometimes be rigid about their thinking and have trouble seeing another perspective. When you're feeling stuck understanding yourself or another person, this meditation can open your eyes to a different perspective of a difficult situation. This meditation is best done seated and may be practiced while sitting on the floor or using two facing chairs.

STEPS:

1. Ground yourself using one of the basic meditations from a previous chapter.

2. Think of a difficult situation you're currently experiencing. Now imagine you're facing either the person you're in conflict with or the part of yourself that's challenging you.

3. Speak out loud to the empty space in front of you, explaining your perspective of the situation. Include your thoughts, emotions, and reasoning.

4. When you finish speaking, complete one mindful breath cycle, noting how your body feels after having spoken your piece.

5. Get up and move into the empty chair or spot on the floor in front of you, facing the spot you previously sat in.

6. Respond to the points you shared a moment ago, as if you're the other person or part of yourself you spoke to. What might they say? How might they feel or think about the situation? What do they need?

CONTINUED

7. After responding, move back to your original chair and continue the dialogue. If you disagree with the person in the empty chair, express it.

8. You may need to go back and forth several times. Remember to complete a mindful breath before moving.

9. You may feel silly or prefer to continue the exercise without moving spots. Resist that urge. Physically moving between spots can actively shift the brain to a deeper insight.

10. When you've finished this exploration, move into a mindful breath practice.

11. Notice whether your body feels different. Has your perspective changed? Do you have a different understanding of the conflict as a result?

Imaginary Stimming

∴ Stress Reduction Exercise   ① *5 minutes*

In a previous meditation, we learned about forcing neurons to wire together by faking a feeling or action (page 149). In chapter 5, we learned about reducing stress through mindful stimming (page 58). But active stimming may be frowned upon in certain situations—you may not be able to table-drum in a business meeting, for example. This exercise may help reduce that unbearable feeling when you need to be still, but the energy is welling up inside you.

STEPS:

1. Practice mindful deep breathing first. This may be enough to physically calm you.

2. If it doesn't, imagine yourself stimming. Visualize what you'd do if you could: bounce your knee, tap the table, pull your hair, make some noise.

3. Visualize what your body is desperate to do. Feel it in your brain as if you're doing it.

4. Breathe into this visualization. Feel the energy pour into the imaginary action and release from your body.

5. Repeat as often as you need.

Where the Heck Is It?

⚹ Mindfulness Exercise   *⏲ As many minutes as you need*

I lose things all the time. They're not really lost; I mindlessly set them down and then forget where they are. The amount of time I waste looking for things is frustrating. Although the best solution is to bring mindful intention to where I place my important things, it's still an exercise in progress. The good news is that people with ADHD are often visual thinkers, and a careful meditation on retracing steps can sometimes locate the lost treasure. The key to this exercise is to practice it as soon as you realize you've misplaced something.

STEPS:

1. Take several deep breaths and relax your body. If you worry too much about finding the item, you'll trigger a stress response in your brain that will make it more difficult to think clearly.

2. Picture the item you're looking for.

3. Try to remember the last place you saw it. Picture yourself in that area. What were you doing in that moment?

4. What did you do next? Did you leave the room or talk to someone? Did something distract you?

5. As best you can, mentally retrace your steps since you last saw the item, going as far back as you can. Then physically go to each location, if possible.

6. If visualizing your steps is not productive, shift your memory to your emotions. What were you feeling in the moment you last saw the item?

7. Go through all your sensations including smell, touch, sound, and taste to help your mind make associations with the memory of the item.

8. If these steps don't lead you to the object the first time, try a basic meditation and focus on your breath or body for a few minutes. Then go back to step 2 and try again.

Generalizing tip: *Routinely putting important items in the same place— for example, keys on a key hook by the door—can help reduce the time you spend searching for things you need every day. If you've kept an infrequently used item in the same location for a long time, resist the urge to reorganize and move it. My mother always called this the "second location syndrome," as she and I both could always remember where an item was originally stored but never the second location we moved it to!*

Wait! Wait!

⁎ *Stress Reduction Exercise*   ⏲ *5 to 20 minutes*

At the doctor's office, in a long line, at a restaurant, or on a delayed flight—the less I know about why I'm being made to wait and wait, the more frustrated I become. Can you relate? Often, if I'm told why I'm waiting—the doctor had an emergency, my friend is stuck in traffic, the airplane has a mechanical issue—then I can replace frustration with compassion and understanding. But we don't always get to know why we're waiting, and the impatience can be brutal, especially for people with ADHD. The next time you're waiting and don't know why, try this meditation to help you through it.

STEPS:

1. When you notice frustration and impatience starting to build while you wait, shift your intention to change your internal state. Start with your breath.

2. With a deep inhalation, acknowledge how you feel right now.

   I'm so frustrated.

   I'm so bored.

   I'm getting angry.

3. Exhale. With your next inhalation, locate where this feeling may be lodged in your body and breathe into that place. As you exhale, relax your body.

4. Inhale and acknowledge how you feel toward the person making you wait.

   This doctor is so rude.

   My friend is so thoughtless.

   I'm never flying this airline again.

5. Exhale.

6. On your next breath cycle, repeat the following:

   I'm not perfect. Sometimes I make unintentional mistakes, and I mean no disrespect by them. Everyone makes mistakes. The person I'm waiting for is not perfect either. They're not purposefully making me wait. This is not about me at all.

7. On your next breath, imagine a warm ball of light filled with compassion and understanding. See yourself sending this ball to the person you're waiting for.

8. Wish them well in their efforts to get to you.

Play-by-Play

The previous meditation practiced sending well wishes to the people who are making us wait, as an effort to ward off our frustration. In addition to frustration, waiting can also cause boredom, which can be equally difficult to tolerate. The next time you're restless waiting somewhere, try the following exercise to pass the time and strengthen your mindfulness skills.

STEPS:

1. Center yourself by sitting or standing upright with your spine straight. Draw a deep, mindful breath into the boredom you're feeling while waiting.

2. As if you're a sports announcer or story narrator, give a play-by-play of the circumstances to an imaginary audience. It may look something like this:

   Our setting is the dermatology practice of Dr. Saunders. There's a glass door on my left and a shiny wooden reception desk to the right. I've been waiting approximately 45 minutes. The waiting room has beige carpet and seven chairs. The receptionist is reaching for the phone. She answers it. Her voice is high and whiny. She places the caller on hold. Across from me, an old man struggles to sit down in the narrow chair . . .

3. If you get distracted from your narration, take a mindful breath and restart. You may find it helpful to stand or shift in your chair.

4. Although this exercise may seem trivial, practicing a play-by-play narration brings your observation skills to the here and now. It also helps pass the time while you're waiting.

Get Down and Dirty

✴ Stress Reduction Exercise   ⏱ *15 minutes*

Studies show that *Mycobacterium vaccae*, a bacteria found in soil, can improve mood, well-being, and digestive health. But when was the last time you played outside in the dirt, breathing it in and getting it underneath your nails? In these days of hand sanitizer, we may be depriving our bodies of some beneficial bacteria. Being outside can also provide a good dose of vitamin D, which is important for bone and immune health. For this meditation, you'll need a patch to dig in (soil or sand) and a willingness to get your hands dirty.

STEPS:

1. Sit, squat, or kneel on your patch of ground.

2. Close your eyes and lift your chin toward the sky. Draw in a breath, and with it, take in the sounds around you.

3. Note how your body feels. What is your comfort level sitting directly on the earth? What is the temperature of the air and the ground?

4. Start digging, being mindful of any sharp rocks or sticks. If the ground is hard, you may need a small trowel to loosen it.

5. As you dig, feel the sensation of the dirt on your fingers and under your nails. Does it feel good, or uncomfortable?

CONTINUED

6. Focus on your breath and the act of digging, as well as any bodily sensations. If you're uncomfortable, feel free to shift your body.

7. Once you're actively digging, your goal is to find the perfect rock. As you encounter rocks, pull them out and inspect them. You'll know the perfect one when you find it. If you don't encounter any rocks, feel free to search for the perfect stick, shell, leaf, or any other natural object you encounter.

8. Once you've found the perfect rock, study it, its shape, size, and color. What made you choose this one? Is it the only one you encountered? Were you rushing this exercise? Did the rock call to you in some way?

9. When you're ready to conclude your adventures in the dirt, bury the perfect rock and any others, returning them to their places in nature.

10. Complete 1 breath cycle, stand, and stretch through another breath cycle.

11. Now, you may wash your hands.

Sharpen Your Vision

⁂ Stress Reduction Exercise   *⏱ 20 minutes*

You may have heard of a "vision board" as a means of manifesting the future of your dreams. The practice of pairing images with your dreams and desires and intentionally setting them to a creative piece has a basis in some of the neuroscience explained in earlier meditations. By visualizing and imagining, you're firing neurons that may help you actively achieve the future you desire. For this meditation, you'll need some supplies: magazines (or a computer with internet and a printer), paper, scissors, markers, and glue.

STEPS:

1. Choose a selection of images and words from the internet or from your magazines that speak to your vision of a desired future. If you're using a computer, print out the images.

2. Spread out the images and supplies on a table that's clear of distractions.

3. You may wish to play music or complete this exercise in silence.

4. Ground yourself in a basic meditation from a previous chapter.

5. When you're ready, begin to cut out the words and images that you've chosen. What do they represent? Visualize yourself as part of this image. How does it feel in your body? What would it mean for your life if this future were true?

6. Hear the sound of the scissors as they cut through the paper. Are there other sounds around you? What might the sounds be in the image you're cutting out?

CONTINUED

7. Feel the scissors in your hand and the texture of the paper. What textures are in the images? Imagine yourself feeling them.

8. Practice mindfulness by moving the paper scraps you don't plan to use into a pile to keep your space tidy.

9. Place the cutout words and images on your paper. Move with purpose. Why are you placing particular images in particular spots? Are you rushing or designing thoughtfully? Take your time.

10. Glue your cutouts to the paper. When you've finished, take in the visual of your creation. Inhale deeply and tell yourself this is a future that has already come true. How does it feel to live this? Reflect.

11. Clean up the project and put away your supplies.

12. Hang your creation where you can glance at it frequently throughout your day.

A Matching Game

⚹ *Focus Exercise*   ⏱ *10 minutes*

When I was little, I used to love playing the matching game. I have a great visual memory, so my poor brother rarely beat me. Playing cards with another person can be fun, but playing alone can be a great time to be mindful and, at the same time, increase your focus and memory skills. For this activity, you'll need a deck of cards.

STEPS:

1. Sit at a table or on the floor with space before you. Ground yourself with a basic mindful breath meditation.

2. Shuffle the card deck well. Place each card facedown so that you have 4 rows of 13 cards.

3. Begin by flipping over two cards. You're searching for cards that match in number and suit color. If there's no match, flip the cards back over.

4. Before flipping over another two cards, breathe and visualize the two cards you just turned over. Close your eyes and imprint the image.

5. Flip over two more cards.

6. Repeat steps 4 and 5 until you find a match. Remove the matching cards and place them aside in a neat pile.

CONTINUED

7. While you play, breathe deeply and rhythmically. Keep your mind on the game. If it wanders to other thoughts, take a breath and return your attention to the cards.

8. If you're having trouble focusing, allow yourself a physical break. Get up and stretch, but first, close your eyes and visualize the placement of the cards you've turned over.

9. Continue playing the game until you've found all the matches.

Generalizing tip: *A solitary game can be great to do at night as part of your wind-down routine. If matching is not your game, consider doing a puzzle or playing solitaire or dominoes. Crocheting and knitting can be similarly relaxing while engaging mindfulness, too.*

What's in a Mnemonic?

⚘ *Mindfulness Exercise*　　　　　🕐 *5 minutes*

Social anxiety is often a friend of ADHD. When we meet someone new, the anxiety of the moment can sometimes cause a stress
response to flood our brains. This makes learning a new acquaintance's name nearly impossible. Mindful mnemonics can come to
your rescue, but it takes intention to practice it. Mnemonics is a
type of association technique that helps you remember by using
imagery or information the brain already knows. Mnemonics
can be used to remember anything, so the next time you meet
someone new, try the following exercise to lock their name into
your brain.

STEPS:

1. As you're meeting someone new, inhale deeply and create an
   intention to be mindful in this interaction. Set your attention on
   this new person.

2. Look at their face and physique. Note anything about them that
   sticks out—the size of their nose, the color of their hair, their
   height, or their eyes.

3. When they say their name, do one of the following:

   a) Associate the name with someone you already know.
      For example, if the name is James, think of James and
      the Giant Peach or James Corden or James your brother.
      Because "neurons that fire together, wire together," this
      association will help your brain recall this particular James
      in the future.

CONTINUED

   b) Associate the most prominent syllable in the name with an image. JAmes to JAil. Then link that image with a physical attribute. For example, maybe James has beady eyes, and you can picture him as a criminal behind bars.

   c) Associate the name with a visual that rhymes with the name. James to aims—picture him aiming a bow and arrow.

This may seem complicated, but it works! Numerous psychological studies have shown that using an association with easily retrievable imagery allows the brain to better recall newly learned information. In addition, by setting an intention to practice your mnemonic device, you may distract your brain from the stress of the social encounter.

4. Be sure to repeat the new acquaintance's name when saying goodbye. Saying "Nice to meet you, James" as you picture poor James in jail will help solidify his name in your brain.

Closing

In Bangkok's Wat Traimit temple, there is a golden statue of the Buddha. In 1955, the arduous task of moving this 10-foot tall, 5-ton plaster statue of Buddha resulted in the statue cracking all over. To the monks' dismay, the statue was thought to be ruined—until they noticed a golden hue emanating from the cracks. Turns out, this statue was made of solid gold and had been covered in plaster 200 years prior to protect it from an invading Burmese army.

Living with ADHD can feel like everyone else's plaster is perfect, but yours is cracked all over. When it comes to executive functioning, emotional regulation, and stress management, our brains are often uncooperative. But without those cracks, we might not see the gold underneath: our brains are also fascinating, resilient, and dynamic. The cracks in our plaster have forced us to become creative problem-solvers, to work harder and smarter, and to be resilient. I hope the meditations in this book have helped deepen your moment-to-moment awareness, given you strategies to help alleviate your ADHD symptoms, and allowed you to see beyond the cracks to develop a deeper compassion for your wonderful monkey mind. Thank you for taking this journey with me.

Resources

ADHD

Boissiere, Phil. *Thriving with Adult ADHD: Skills to Strengthen Executive Functioning*. Althea Press, 2018.

Safren, Steven A., Susan E. Sprich, Carol A. Perlman, and Michael W. Otto. *Mastering Your Adult ADHD: A Cognitive-Behavioral Treatment Program*. Oxford University Press, 2017.

Sarkis, Stephanie M. *10 Simple Solutions to Adult ADD*. New Harbinger Publications, 2011.

Tuckman, Ari. *More Attention, Less Deficit: Success Strategies for Adults with ADHD*. Specialty Press, 2009.

Mindfulness

Chödrön, Pema. *Compassion Cards: Teachings for Awakening the Heart in Everyday Life*. Shambhala, 2016.

Economou, Peter. *Mindfulness Workbook for Beginners*. Rockridge Press, 2021.

Goleman, Daniel. *Emotional Intelligence*. Random House Publishing Group, 2005.

Kabat-Zinn, Jon. *Full Catastrophe Living*. Little, Brown Book Group, 2013.

van der Kolk, Bessel. *The Body Keeps the Score*. Penguin Publishing Group, 2015.

References

Andrews-Hanna, Jessica. "The Brain's Default Network and Its Adaptive
Role in Internal Mentation." *Neuroscientist* 18, no. 3 (2012): 251–70. doi.
org/10.1177/1073858411403316.

Beck, Judith S. *Cognitive Therapy: Basics and Beyond*. New York: Guilford
Press, 1995.

Children and Adults with Attention-Deficit/Hyperactivity Disorder. "ADHD
and Co-occuring Conditions." Accessed September 8, 2021. CHADD.org
/about-adhd/co-occuring-conditions.

Chödrön, Pema. *The Wisdom of No Escape and the Path of Loving-Kindness*.
Boston: Shambhala Publications, 1991.

Coué, Émile. *Self-Mastery through Conscious Autosuggestion*. London:
Taylor & Francis, 1920.

Curran, Linda, Peter Levine, Janina Fisher, Stephen Porges, et al. Treating
Complex Trauma: Beyond Competency. PESI. Accessed September 8,
2021. Catalog.PESI.com/sales/bh_c_001376evg_treatingcomplextrauma
_organic-127314.

Delehanty, Hugh. "The Science of Meditation." *Mindful*. December 13, 2017.
Mindful.org/meditators-under-the-microscope.

Deng, Francis. "Mnemonics, Not Magic: How to Accomplish Feats of
Memory." *The Harvard Brain*. Accessed September 8, 2021.
HCS.Harvard.edu/brain/featured/Deng_Mnemonics.

Dumont, Theron Q. *The Power of Concentration*. Chicago: Advanced
Thought Publishing, 1918.

Gladwell, Malcolm. *Outliers: The Story of Success*. New York: Little,
Brown, 2008.

Goleman, Daniel, and Richard J. Davidson. *Altered Traits: Science Reveals How Meditation Changes Your Mind, Brain, and Body*. New York: Avery, 2017.

Greenberger, Dennis, and Christine A. Padesky. *Mind over Mood: A Cognitive Therapy Treatment Manual for Clients*. New York: Guilford Press, 1995.

Hanh, Thich Nhat. *Peace Is in Every Step: The Path of Mindfulness in Every day Life*. New York: Bantam Books, 1991.

Harada, Hiroki, Hideki Kashiwadani, Yuichi Kanmura, and Tomoyuki Kuwaki. "Linalool Odor-Induced Anxiolytic Effects in Mice." *Frontiers in Behavioral Neuroscience* 12 (October 2018): 241. doi.org/10.3389/fnbeh.2018.00241.

IGEA Brain, Spine & Orthopedics. "Becoming Mindful of the Brain and Its Functions." May 9, 2017. IGEANeuro.com/blog/becoming-mindful -brain-functions.

Jellinek, Michael. "Don't Let ADHD Crush Children's Self-Esteem." *Clinical Psychiatry News*, May 2010. MDEdge.com/psychiatry/article/23971/pediatrics /dont-let-adhd-crush-childrens-self-esteem.

Kabat-Zinn, Jon. *Full Catastrophe Living: Using the Wisdom of Your Body and Mind to Face Stress, Pain, and Illness*. Rev. ed. New York: Bantam Books, 2013.

Keysers, Christian, and Valeria Gazzola. "Hebbian Learning and Predictive Mirror Neurons for Actions, Sensations and Emotions." *Philosophical Transactions of the Royal Society B: Biological Sciences* 369, no. 1644 (June 2014): 20130175. doi.org/10.1098/rstb.2013.0175.

Khasawneh, Ahmad H., Richard J. Garling, and Carolyn A. Harris. "Cerebro-spinal Fluid Circulation: What Do We Know and How Do We Know It?" *Brain Circulation* 4, no. 1 (2018): 14–18. doi.org/10.4103/bc.BC_3_18.

Krpan, Katherine M., Ethan Kross, Marc G. Berman, Patricia J. Deldin, Mary K. Askren, and John Jonides. "An Everyday Activity as a Treatment for Depression: The Benefits of Expressive Writing for People Diagnosed with Major Depressive Disorder." *Journal of Affective Disorders* 150, no. 3 (September 2013): 1148–51. doi.org/10.1016/j.jad.2013.05.065.

Lunsford-Avery, Jessica R., and Scott H. Kollins. "Editorial Perspective: Delayed Circadian Rhythm Phase; A Cause of Late-Onset Attention-Deficit/Hyperactivity Disorder among Adolescents?" *Journal of Child Psychology and Psychiatry* 59, no. 12 (December 2018): 1248–51. doi.org/10.1111/jcpp.12956.

Lutz, Antoine, Amishi P. Jha, John D. Dunne, and Clifford D. Saron. "Investigating the Phenomenological Matrix of Mindfulness-Related Practices from a Neurocognitive Perspective." *American Psychologist* 70, no. 7 (October 2015): 632–58. doi.org/10.1037/a0039585.

MacGill, Markus. "What Is the Link between Love and Oxytocin?" *Medical News Today.* September 4, 2017. MedicalNewsToday.com /articles/275795.

Meng, Xiao, Ya Li, Sha Li, Yue Zhou, Ren-You Gan, Dong-Ping Xu, and Hua-Bin Li. "Dietary Sources and Bioactivities of Melatonin." *Nutrients* 9, no. 4 (April 2017): 367. doi.org/10.3390/nu9040367.

Mindful Staff. "The Science of Mindfulness." *Mindful.* September 7, 2020. Mindful.org/the-science-of-mindfulness.

Mostajeran, Fariba, Jessica Krzikawski, Frank Steinicke, and Simone Kühn. "Effects of Exposure to Immersive Videos and Photo Slideshows of Forest and Urban Environments." *Scientific Reports* 11 (2021): 3994. doi.org/10.1038/s41598-021-83277-y.

Neff, Kristin. "Self-Compassion." By James Baraz. Insight Meditation Community of Berkeley. March 7, 2013. Audio, 54:25. DharmaSeed.org/talks/18768/?access_key=Fmc7WnjXhU.

Owens Viani, Lisa. "Good posture is Important for Physical and Mental Health." *SF State News*. December 15, 2017. news.SFSU.edu /news-story/good-posture-important-physical-and-mental-health.

Patel, Poulam M., Sreyneang Sim, D. O. O'Donnell, Andrew Protheroe, Debbie Beirne, A. Stanley, J. M. Tourani, et al. "An Evaluation of a Preparation of *Mycobacterium vaccae* (SRL172) as an Immunotherapeutic Agent in Renal Cancer." *European Journal of Cancer* 44, no. 2 (January 2008): 216–23. doi.org/10.1016/j.ejca.2007.11.003.

Poissant, Hélène, Adrianna Mendrek, Nadine Talbot, Bassam Khoury, and Jennifer Nolan. "Behavioral and Cognitive Impacts of Mindfulness-Based Interventions on Adults with Attention-Deficit Hyperactivity Disorder: A Systematic Review." *Behavioural Neurology* 2019 (April 2019): 1–16. doi. org/10.1155/2019/5682050.

Quinn, Daley. "What Are Dantian? The Energy Centers of Chinese Medicine." *Healthline*. December 28, 2020. Healthline.com/health/dantian.

Reber, Stefan O., Philip H. Siebler, Nina S. Donner, James T. Morton, David G. Smith, Jared M. Kopelman, Kenneth R. Lowe, et al. "Immunization with a Heat-Killed Preparation of the Environmental Bacterium *Mycobacterium vaccae* Promotes Stress Resilience in Mice." *Proceedings of the National Academy of Sciences of the United States of America* 113, no. 22 (May 2016): e3130–39. doi.org/10.1073/pnas.1600324113.

Shukla, Aditya. "The Scientific Truth behind 'Fake it till you make it.'" *Cognition Today*. Last updated December 9, 2020. CognitionToday .com/the-scientific-truth-behind-fake-it-till-you-make-it.

Smalley, Susan L., and Diana Winston. *Fully Present: The Science, Art, and Practice of Mindfulness*. N.p.: Da Capo Lifelong, 2010.

Stefan, Simona Ioana, and Stefan G. Hofmann. "Integrating Metta into CBT: How Loving Kindness and Compassion Meditation Can Enhance CBT for Treating Anxiety and Depression." *Clinical Psychology in Europe* 1, no. 3 (September 2019): e32941. doi.org/10.32872/cpe.v1i3.32941.

Tirch, Dennis, Laura R. Silberstein, and Russell L. Kolts. *Buddhist Psychology and Cognitive-Behavioral Therapy: A Clinician's Guide*. New York: Guilford Press, 2016.

Umejima, Keita, Takuya Ibaraki, Takahiro Yamazaki, and Kuniyoshi L. Sakai. "Paper Notebooks vs. Mobile Devices: Brain Activation Differences during Memory Retrieval." *Frontiers in Behavioral Neuroscience* 15 (March 2021). doi.org/10.3389/fnbeh .2021.634158.

van der Kolk, Bessel A. *The Body Keeps the Score: Brain, Mind, and Body in the Healing of Trauma*. New York: Penguin Books, 2014.

Wapner, Jessica. "Vision and Breathing May Be the Secrets to Surviving 2020." *Scientific American*. November 16, 2020. ScientificAmerican.com/article/vision-and-breathing-may-be-the -secrets-to-surviving-2020.

Xue, Jiaming, Yun Zhang, Ying Huang. "A Meta-Analytic Investigation of the Impact of Mindfulness-Based Interventions on ADHD Symptoms." *Medicine* 98, no. 23 (June 2019): e15957. doi.org/10.1097 /MD.0000000000015957.

Zylowska, Lidia. *The Mindfulness Prescription for Adult ADHD: An Eight-Step Program for Strengthening Attention, Managing Emotions, and Achieving Your Goals*. Boston: Trumpeter, 2012.

Index

Acknowledgments

This endeavor owes thanks to the grounding friendships of Rebecca Johnson, Leanne Battelle, Cameron Urban, Sarah Margulies, Sarah Benedetto, Sarah Squiers, Catherine Ludbrook, Janique Pécarrère, Laurie Fried, Kim Cronin, Amy Cardamone, Sally Pla, Cami Loft, Dana Delaney, Lauren Cargill, Jennifer Lynn Alvarez, Nikki Garcia, Shells Legoullon, Lisa B. Schulman, Kristyn Michael, James Sarcia, Janet Silcox, and my family. Great thanks to my editors Jed Bickman and Patty Consolazio and the team at Rockridge Press for the opportunity to write these meditations during a time of life when mindfulness was the very thing I needed.

About the Author

Merriam Sarcia Saunders, LMFT, is a professor and psychotherapist specializing in ADHD. She's the author of the acclaimed ADHD children's books *My Whirling, Twirling Motor*; *My Wandering, Dreaming Mind*; and *Trouble with a Tiny T*. She is also the author of the nonfiction *Divorce and the ADHD, Autistic, Anxious Child* and is a regular contributor to *ADDitude* magazine. She cofounded ANovelMind.com, a resource for mental health in children's books. Merriam is a certified ADHD clinical services provider, mindfulness-informed clinician, clinical trauma professional, and divorce mediator. Visit MerriamSaunders.com.

CPSIA information can be obtained
at www.ICGtesting.com
Printed in the USA
JSHW041246250222
23359JS00002B/3